Questions & Answers

GW00708105

ECONOMICS

Alan Gully MSc
Senior Lecturer in Economics
Middlesex Polytechnic

Longman
London and New York

Longman Group Limited, London

Associated companies, branches and representatives
throughout the world

Published in the United States of America
by Longman Inc., New York

First published 1980

 British Library Cataloguing in Publication Data

Gully, Alan
Economics. - (Questions and Answers).
1. Economics - Problems, exercises, etc.
1. Title II. Series
330 .076 HB171.5   78-41317

ISBN 0-582-41174-2

Printed in Hong Kong by
Wilture Enterprises (International) Ltd

I am grateful to my wife, Therese, for her patience and
perseverence in typing the many drafts of the manuscript.

A.G. Gully

Contents

Introduction

The purpose of this book is to help students who are studying economics. Almost all business studies and professional accountancy courses include economics as an examinable subject. Economic examinations at an intermediate level require an analytic as well as a descriptive approach to the subject. It is this analytic part that often causes great difficulty for students who attempt to learn rather than understand economics. The author, who is an experienced economics lecturer and examiner, has brought together a wide range of intermediate economics questions that will help the student test his/her knowledge of the subject. The answers have been skilfully written so the student can understand the requirements of the questions and provide some indication of the standard required to achieve high marks in the examination. A special appendix on numerical economic questions has been included because of the difficulty many students have in answering this type of question. Although a basic knowledge of economics is necessary the detailed answers ensure that students will be capable of understanding all the questions in this book. Most economics textbooks include questions but few provide the detailed answers that the student needs. This book provides economics students with a means of testing, assessing and improving their knowledge of economics in preparation for examinations.

How to use this book

This book has been written to help you with the essential practice of answering questions and checking the answer with a detailed model answer. Therefore as each section is covered in the teaching programme you can then turn to the relevant section in this book and practice answering questions. It is important not to look at the answer until the question has been attempted. Then compare your answer with the detail and layout of the model answer. Locate any mistakes you may have made and ensure that you understand why you were wrong. If you have made a lot of mistakes study the subject area carefully and try the questions again. Examinations consist of questions that have to be answered within a certain time allowance. Accordingly, you must time yourself when answering practice questions and get used to working quickly and neatly. Appendix I contains numerical economics questions and answers specially written for students who have difficulty with this aspect of the subject. Appendix II explains how to prepare for economics examinations and gives some hints that will help you succeed in the examination.

To
JONATHAN
and
TIMOTHY

Question 1   Demand   Answer page 16

Under what conditions will people buy more of a product the price of which has risen?

Question 2   Supply   Answer page 21

What is the justification for drawing the supply curve of a commodity so as to suggest that larger quantities are offered for sale at higher prices?

Question 3   Price Determination   Answer page 22

Given the hypothetical data below concerning the U.K. beef market per week in 1980:

a) Calculate the equilibrium price and quantity if the market only included the home demand. Explain your calculation.
b) Now take account of home and export demand to calculate the new equilibrium price and quantity. Explain your calculation and state the amount exported.
c) Discuss the effect of a fall in the price of other meat (for domestic consumption only) on the quantity of beef exported.

Price (p per lb)	Supply (lbs)	Home Demand (lbs)	Export demand (lbs)
60	160	260	110
80	180	230	90
100	200	200	70
120	220	170	50
140	240	140	30

Question 4 **Price Elasticity** Answer page 23

Examine from the point of view of revenue raised and impact on consumers and producers, the effect of imposing a tax on a commodity when demand for it is a) elastic, b) inelastic over the appropriate price range.

Question 5 **Price Controls** Answer page 26

What would you expect to be the economic consequences of a price system in which some prices were fixed by law and not by supply and demand in a free market?

Question 6 **Agricultural Policy** Answer page 28

Discuss the potential effects of government intervention in the agricultural sector to stabilize a) food prices, b) farmers' incomes, by the establishment of a buffer stock.

Question 7 **Business Organisation** Answer page 31

To what extent has the market economy given way to the corporate economy?

Question 8   Sources of Finance   Answer page 32

What are the main sources of company finance? How are their relative costs affected by inflation?

Question 9   Business Objectives   Answer page 34

What grounds are there for asserting that firms are not profit maximisers ?

Question 10   Location of Industry   Answer page 36

What factors should be considered in deciding where a particular firm should site a factory?

Question 11   Costs   Answer page 37

Fixed costs do not arise in the long run and are irrelevant in the short run. Explain.

Answer page 39

Question 12   Optimal Factor Mix

How should a firm decide in what proportion to combine the factors of production it employs?

Answer page 40

Question 13   Returns to Scale/Factor

Distinguish clearly between returns to scale and returns to a factor. What is the relationship between these returns and the firm's cost curves?

Answer page 42

Question 14   Investment Criteria

A firm is considering the purchase of a new machine. Its initial cost is £1,000 and it is expected to earn a net return of £400 at the end of the next three years, after which it is to be scrapped at zero cost.
a) Advise the firm on the profitability of the project, if the cost of capital is 10%.
b) If the firm is taken over by a larger company with access to funds at 8% would your answer be affected?

Period (n)		0	1	2	3
Discount factor	r = 10%	1.0	.909	.826	.751
Discount factor	r = 8%	1.0	.926	.857	.794

Answer page 43

Question 15   Perfect Competition

Examine the short and long-run consequences for the perfectly competitive firm and industry of imposing a lump-sum tax on each firm.

Question 16   Imperfect Competition   **Answer page 45**

What economic factors influence the level of advertising expenditure and its influence in different markets?

Question 17   Monopoly   **Answer page 47**

A monopolist has the following information available:

Price £	Output (units)	Total Cost £
10	10	170
9	20	190
8	30	215
7	40	250
6	50	300
5	60	370

Note - output is only produced in batches of 10 units.

As economic adviser to the monopolist you are required to determine:

i)   the profit maximising level of output.
ii)   the price elasticity of demand at this point.
iii) the output level at which price equals average cost.
iv)   using your results to (i) and (iii) briefly indicate why mono-poly is considered evil.

Question 18   Price Discrimination   **Answer page 48**

Show that a monopolist may obtain higher profits if he can divide his customers into separate markets.

Question 19   Restrictive Practices   Answer page 51

Discuss the justification for the difference in emphasis in the
U.K. between monopoly and merger policy on the one hand and
restrictive trade practices on the other.

Question 20   Economic Concentration   Answer page 53

How is it possible to measure monopoly power?

Question 21   Nationalised Industries   Answer page 55

'The aims of pricing policy in the Nationalised Industries should
be that the consumer should pay the true costs of the goods and
services he consumes.' Discuss.

Question 22   Industrial Structure   Answer page 57

'Restructuring the economy should be left to market forces'.
Discuss this statement in the light of the operation of the National
Enterprise Board.

What factors determine the elasticity of demand for a
factor of production?

'It is immobility of capital rather than immobility of labour
which accounts for regional variations in unemployment.'
Discuss.

What effects do trade unions have on wages in an industry?

'The price of cinema seats is high because the demand for
cinema seats is high.'
'The price of cinema seats is high because the price of land
is high.'
Comment on these two statements.

Question 27   Wage Controls   Answer page 68

Discuss the economic consequences of government legislation to establish a minimum wage in a particular industry.

Question 28   Measuring National Income   Answer page 70

What do you understand by the term "National Income"? Explain the possible ways in which it may be measured.

Question 29   Interpreting National Income   Answer page 72

What are the main objections to using increases in Gross Domestic Product as an index of increases in Social Welfare?

Question 30   Consumption   Answer page 74

What factors affect the aggregate level of consumption expenditure?

Question 31   Investment   Answer page 76

What factors determine the level of aggregage business investment?

Question 32   Income Determination   Answer page 78

At the equilibrium level of income in an economy, aggregate expenditure is equal to aggregate production. In the National Income Accounts aggregate expenditure always equals aggregate output. Are we therefore always in equilibrium ?

Question 33   Multiplier   Answer page 79

Analyse the effects of an increase in the level of investment in an economy a) with substantial unemployment and b) with full employment.

Question 34   Fiscal Policy   Answer page 81

To what extent can fluctuations in economic activity be regulated solely by varying the size of the government's budget deficit or surplus?

Question 35   **Nature and Functions of Money**   Answer page 84

'It is impossible to agree on a single functional definition of
money'. Discuss

Question 36   **Central Bank**   Answer page 86

How effectively can the Bank of England control the supply of
money?

Question 37   **Commercial Banks**   Answer page 89

'Commercial banks may only lend what has been deposited
with them and therefore cannot create money'. Discuss.

Question 38   **Liquidity Preference**   Answer page 91

Discuss the effect of inflation on the demand for money.

Question 39   **Monetary Policy**   Answer page 92

'It is possible to control either the stock of money or the rate of interest, but not both.' Explain and discuss.

Question 40   **National Debt**   Answer page 94

Is the National Debt a burden?

Question 41   **Comparative Advantage**   Answer page 95

Is it true that a country can only gain from trade if another country loses?

Question 42   **Balance of Payments Accounts**   Answer page 97

'Britain's balance of payments deficit in 1974 was the highest yet.'
'The balance of payments must always balance.'
Reconcile these two statements.

How do fluctuations in the foreign exchange rate arise? What is the case for trying to stabilise this rate?

Are depreciation and deflation equivalent methods of improving the balance of payments?

Evaluate the role of the International Monetary Fund in the post-war world economy.

'The unemployment problem cannot be solved simply by stimulating aggregate demand.' Discuss.

Question 47   Inflation   Answer page 106

'Demand - pull and cost - push are merely different names for the
same type of inflation, therefore either monetary contraction or
prices and incomes policies may be used to eliminate this problem.'
Discuss.

Question 48   Phillips Curve   Answer page 111

Is there a trade-off between inflation and unemployment?

Question 49   Keynesianism and Monetarism   Answer page 114

'Keynesian policies are incompatible with price stability.'
'Monetarists policies are incompatible with full employment.'
Discuss the validity of these two statements.

Question 50   Management of the Economy   Answer page 116

Discuss the case for fixed rules versus discretionary macroeconomic
stabilization policies.

Question 51   **Trade Cycle**   **Answer page 118**

To what extent is volatility of investment expenditure the cause of instability in an economy?

Question 52   **Economic Growth**   **Answer page 120**

Discuss the role of investment in the process of economic growth.

Question 53   **Economic Development**   **Answer page 122**

'Since modern technology has been developed for capital-rich economies where labour is more fully employed and expensive, developing economies are forced either to adopt a technology inappropriate to their factor endowments or to use inefficient traditional techniques'. Do you agree?

Question 54   **Income Distribution**   **Answer page 123**

The case for a social dividend or negative income tax to reduce the degree of inequality in the distribution of income founders upon the problem of incentives'. Discuss.

Question 55   Population   Answer page 126

What is the relationship between economic growth and the growth
of population?

Question 56   Poverty   Answer page 128

"The solution to the problem of poverty is a national minimum
wage". Critically discuss.

Question 57   Resource Depletion   Answer page 131

How would you expect a market system to adjust to the approaching
depletion of a natural resource?

The law of demand states that as the price of a good rises, so less of that commodity will be purchased. This question, then, is seeking special circumstances when this law is broken. In order to find these we must analyse the two effects of a price change. The substitution effect is concerned with changes in relative prices, while the income effect is concerned with changes in real income or purchasing power.

For a normal good these two factors act in the same direction. A rise in the price of a commodity increases its price relative to other commodities and causes other goods to be substituted for it. A rise in the price of a commodity also reduces the individual's real income in as much as he is now unable to purchase the same amount of commodities as before the price rise. Usually we expect this reduction in real income to cause a fall in demand. Hence both the income and substitution effects operate in the same direction causing less of a commodity to be purchased when its price rises. The demand curve for such a commodity therefore slopes downwards as predicted by the law of demand.

For inferior goods a fall in income is associated with a larger quantity being demanded. So the income effect of a price change is opposite to that of a normal good. Thus the income and substitution effects act in opposing directions. However the Demand curve would still slope downwards while the substitution effect was greater than the income effect. Only when the income effect is greater than the substitution effect (and acts in the opposite direction) will the demand curve slope upwards. In this case the commodity is called a Giffen good.

This situation is illustrated in Figure (1) which employs indifference theory[1] for two commodities W and X. Given the

---

[1] There are three general approaches to the analysis of demand: indifference theory, marginal utility theory, and revealed preference theory. Students who are familiar with the first technique should read on. Those who have been taught using the second approach may pass on to Answer 1(a). The last method is employed in Answer 1(b).

individual's income Y and initial prices P_w and P_x, we may construct his initial budget line FE, reflecting combinations of the two goods he could just afford to purchase if he spent all his income. Note that OF represents the amount of W he could buy if he purchased none of X.

i.e.

$$OF = \frac{Y}{P_w}$$

Similarly $$OE = \frac{Y}{P_x}$$

Fig. 1

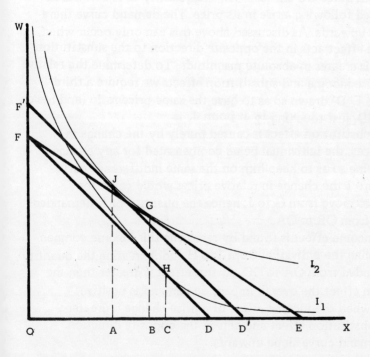

Given also a set of convex indifference curves, each reflecting combinations of the two goods which yield equal satisfaction, then the highest indifference curve the individual can attain within his fixed budget will be one such as I_2 which just touches the budget line at point G. Here the amount of X purchased is OB, which is his utility maximising quantity of X demanded at the price P_x, given constant values for Y and P_w.

Now consider the effect of a rise in the price of X to P_x^1. This causes the budget line to rotate inwards to FD. By the same reasoning as above

$$OD = \frac{Y}{P_x^1}$$

The highest indifference curve he can now attain is I_1, which just touches the new budget line at H, where an amount OC of X is purchased. Since OC exceeds OB, the quantity of X demanded has increased following a rise in its price. The demand curve therefore slopes upwards. As discussed above this can only occur when the income effect acts in the opposite direction to the substitution effect and is greater in absolute magnitude. To determine the relative sizes of these income and substitution effects we require a third budget line F′ D′ drawn so as to have the same price ratio (and hence slope) as GD, just touching I_2 at point J.

The substitution effect is caused purely by the change in relative prices, the individual being compensated for any change in real income so as to keep him on the same indifference curve I_2. In Figure 1 the change in relative prices would cause the individual to move from G to J, hence the quantity of X demanded would fall from OB to OA.

The income effect is found by removing this income compensation, forcing the individual from J to H and increasing the quantity of X demanded from OA to OC. As this effect is greater than the substitution effect the overall impact on demand is positive. Thus only when the income effect of a price change is greater than the substitution effect and acts in the opposite direction will the demand curve slope upwards.

Answer 1(a)

If successive increments of a commodity yield lower levels of utility (i.e. the "law of diminishing marginal utility" holds) then the consumer should purchase units of the good until the utility derived from the last marginal unit is equal to the market price. If there are only two commodities, X and W, then the consumer would attain a utility maximising equilibrium where:

$$\frac{MU_X}{P_X} = \frac{MU_W}{P_W}$$

MU_X and MU_W are the marginal utilities of X and W, and P_X, P_W are their prices.

If the price of X rises to P_X' , and the marginal utilities are unaffected, then clearly:

$$\frac{MU_X}{P_X'} < \frac{MU_W}{P_W}$$

Therefore the consumer must adjust his consumption pattern to achieve a new utility maximising equilibrium. This could be achieved by purchasing less of X and more of W, thus reducing MU_X and increasing MU_W, until equilibrium is restored. This is the substitution effect, operating through changes in relative prices.

As the price of X has risen the consumer's real purchasing power has fallen, so that there will also be an income effect. He cannot afford to purchase the same quantities of X and W as he did previously, and so must reduce his consumption of one or both goods. The fall in income may increase the marginal utility of X relative to W, so that when the income effect exceeds the substitution effect, the price rise leads to a situation where:

$$\frac{MU_X}{P_X'} > \frac{MU_W}{P_W}$$

In this case the consumer would now purchase more of X and less of W to attain equilibrium. This may occur when good X represents a large part of total expenditure and is also (obviously) an inferior good. Only in these extreme conditions would a price rise lead to an increase in demand for the commodity.

Answer 1(b)

This situation is represented in Fig. 1' which employs revealed preference theory for two commodities, X and W. Given the individual's income Y and the initial prices, P_X and P_W, we may construct his initial budget line FE, reflecting combinations of the two goods he could just afford to purchase if he spent all his income. Suppose the consumer is observed to purchase a combination of the two goods represented by point A. Now suppose the price of X rises to P_X'. This causes the budget line to rotate inwards to FD. If the new combination chosen is represented by point C then the quantity of X increases following the price rise. It is possible to analyse income and substitution effects as follows. Suppose as the price of X rose the individual was given an increase in income to allow him to purchase the original combination A. With the new set of relative prices the budget line rotates about A to F'D'. The individual will choose a combination such as B. As X has become relatively more expensive we expect this substitution effect to cause him to reduce his purchases of X from, say, OH to OG. If we now

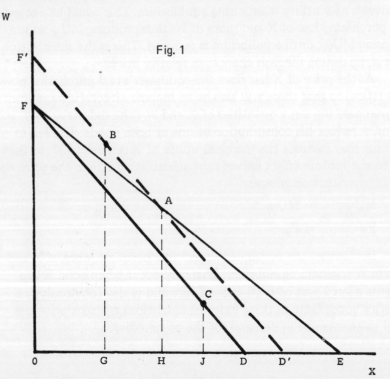

Fig. 1

reduce the consumer's money income to its original level the budget line moves inward to FD. If he now purchases a combination such as C then the increase in X from OG to OJ is due to the income effect. Note in this case the income effect is greater than the substitution effect, and operates in the opposite direction. Only when this condition holds will the demand curve slope upwards, and more of the commodity will be purchased following a rise in its price.

Answer 2 **Supply** Question page 1

The supply curve of a competitive firm is its marginal cost curve above the minimum of its average variable cost, and zero below that position. In the short-run, marginal costs are usually consid ered to be "U" shaped due to the law of diminishing returns to a factor[1]. So, in conjunction with the assumption that factor prices do not fall as their usage increases, the law of diminishing returns provides the justification for the upward slope of a firm's short-run supply curve.

Since the short-run supply curve for a competitive industry is the horizontal sum of each individual firm's supply curves, it too slopes upwards. Indeed, it may slope more steeply, for if all firms increase factor use there may be upward pressure on factor prices, increasing costs still further.

In the long-run the shape of the marginal and average cost curves depends on many considerations. Again, as the output of the industry is expanded higher prices may have to be paid to the factors of production to induce an increased availability in this particular industry. Also, as output is expanded there may be an adverse effect on costs for other firms in this or another industry due to increased pollution, noise or congestion of transport facilities. These will force costs up and make the long-run supply curve slope upwards more steeply.

On the other hand as the level of output expands the firm may be able to use some highly indivisible factor of production to reduce its costs (e.g. buying its own computer). Or the growth of an industry could lead to development of subsidiary industries sited locally, reducing transport costs. These factors would tend to reduce the steepness of the long-run supply curve of the firm and industry or even cause it to be forward falling (downward sloping) in some instances.

These long-run factors which influence costs are termed economies or dis-economies of scale. As we have seen above, they may be either internal (due to say rising input prices or indivisibilities), or external (pollution). As these may either increase or decrease long-run costs there is less of a case for drawing an upward sloping supply curve in the long-run than there is in the short-run.

1. See the answer to Q.13 for further elaboration.

....

| **Answer 3** | **Price Determination** | **Question page 1** |

....

a) Equilibrium occurs when demand equals supply. Home demand is just sufficient to purchase the available supply at a price of 100p, when 200 lbs. is purchased. Comparison of home demand figures with supply shows excess demand at a price of 80p. or less, excess supply at 120 p. or more. In circumstances of excess demand we expect unsatisfied customers to bid the price of beef upwards. When there is excess supply farmers will be left with perishable unsold stocks and will ask lower prices for them.

b) Adding export demand to the domestic demand gives the following total demand schedule.

Price	P	60	80	100	120	140
Total demand	Q	370	320	270	220	170

By comparison with the supply schedule we see the equilibrium price is raised to 120p. Total demand is 220 lbs. of which 50 lbs. is exported. Below the equilibrium price excess demand would put upward pressure on the price. Similarly below the equilibrium price the excess supply would exert downward pressure on price.

c) If the price of other domestically consumed meat fell this would cause the home demand schedule to shift inwards as people substituted some other cheaper meat for beef from D_h to D'_h in Fig. 2. This would also shift the total demand curve for beef inwards from D_t to D'_t, causing an excess supply situation at P_1. The resulting fall in price from P_1 to P_2 would stimulate export demand from X_1 to X_2 and partially offset the fall in home demand. Fig. 2 shows this situation.

Fig. 2

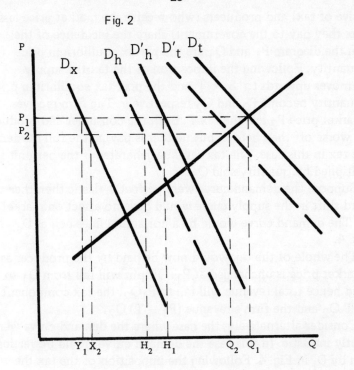

By definition, the supply schedule shows the quantity of a
commodity firms are willing to supply at alternative market
prices. Placing a tax on the commodity shifts this supply curve
upwards by the full amount of the tax, for after payment of the
tax the firm receives exactly the same amount per unit as they had
before the tax was imposed, and would therefore be willing to
supply the same quantity. What happens to the market price
depends not only on the shift of the supply curve but also upon
demand conditions. If the demand curve slopes downwards and
supply upwards as is the usual case, shown in Fig. 3, then the
market price rises, but by less than the amount of the tax, indicating that both consumers (who must pay the higher market price

inclusive of tax) and producers (who receive the market price less the tax they pay to the government) share the incidence of the tax. In the diagram P_1 and Q_1 are the pretax equilibrium price and quantity. Following the imposition of the tax the supply curve moves upwards to $S + T$ and the post-tax equilibrium price and quantity become P_2 and Q_2 respectively. The firm receives the market price P_2 less the tax T. Both the consumer and producer are worse off than before, but neither is paying the full burden of the tax in this case. The tax revenue generated is the per unit tax T multiplied by quantity sold Q_2.

Suppose the demand curve were perfectly elastic then the upward shift in the supply curve would have no effect on market price. The demand curve would be a horizontal line such as D_e in Fig. 4.

The whole of the tax would now be paid by the producer as the market price is unchanged at P_1. Output will fall from Q_1 to Q_2 and hence total revenue will fall to $P_1 Q_2$, the tax component being $T.Q_2$ and the firm's revenue $(P_1 - T) Q_2$.

Consider alternatively, the case where the demand curve were perfectly inelastic. In this case the demand curve would be vertical, shown by D_i in Fig. 4. Following the imposition of the tax the

Fig. 3

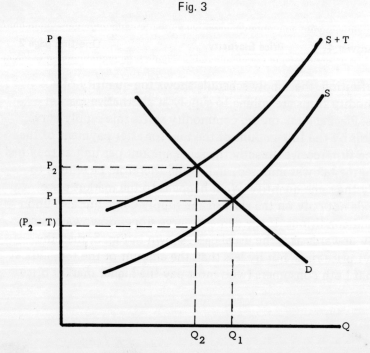

Fig. 4

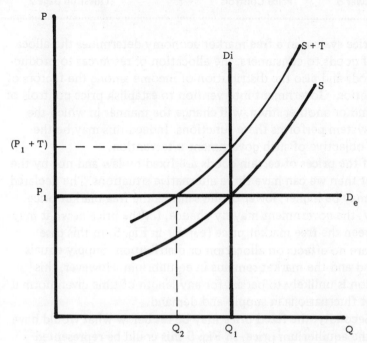

market price would rise by the full amount of the tax to $P_1 + T$ and exactly the same quantity would be sold. The consumer would therefore bear the full burden of the tax. The firm receives the same post-tax revenue as previously while the tax revenue equals $T.Q_1$.

We can conclude that the more elastic is the demand curve, the more the incidence of taxation falls on the producer. Conversely, the less elastic is the demand curve the more the incidence of taxation falls on the consumer. Tax revenue generated is higher when the demand curve is inelastic, and lower when it is elastic.

The price system in a free market economy determines the allocation of goods to consumers, the allocation of resources to producing goods and also the distribution of income among the factors of
production. Government intervention to establish price controls of
one kind or another, then, will change the manner in which the
price system performs these functions. Indeed this may be the
prime objective of such government intervention.

   If the prices of certain goods are fixed by law and not by the
market then we can have three alternative situations. The declared
price may be higher, lower or the same as the free market price.
Firstly, the government may by chance, fix the price at what may
have been the free market price (e.g. P_1 in Fig. 5. In this case
there are no effects on allocation or distribution. Supply equals
demand and the market remains in equilibrium. However, this
situation is unlikely to persist for any length of time given normal
market fluctuations in supply and demand.

   Secondly, the fixed price may be set below what would have
been the equilibrium price. In Fig. 5 this could be represented
by P_2. Here producers have moved back down their supply curve
to offer a reduced quantity for sale, whereas consumers have
moved further down the demand curve wanting to purchase more
of the good. This indicates that at price P_2 demand exceeds supply
and a shortage of the commodity emerges. The extent of their
excess demand is indicated on Fig. 5. The available supply must
be allocated to customers in one of several ways: according to the
seller's preferences (regular customers) or on a "first come first
served" basis (lengthy queues), or rationed by governments
according to their chosen criterion.

   The existence of a pool of unsatisfied purchasers willing to
pay more than the legal price for the commodity usually gives
rise to the development of a Black Market, where the commodity
is sold illegally at a higher price than the legal maximum. This
may defeat the objectives of the price legalisation, assuming that
these were to control prices, with a view to allocating the good to
some purchasers who could not afford the higher free market
price, or ration a scarce product fairly. If the aim of the government was to reduce overall production of the good and free
resources for other uses then in this it would be successful (e.g.

Fig. 5

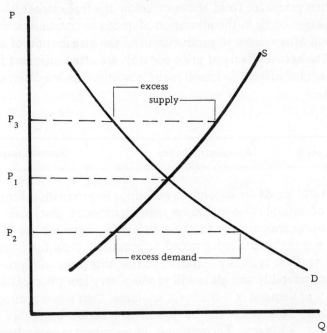

wartime price controls on consumer goods favoured military goods
programme.)

The third possibility we may consider is when the government
fixes the price above the equilibrium. In such a situation the producers are willing to offer an increased supply and move up their
supply curve. However some potential purchasers are put off by
the higher price and move back their demand curve. Thus at price
P₃ there is an excess supply (glut) and producers are left with
unsold stocks of the commodity. This suggests that producers
will try to use various tactics such as free offers or better after-
sales service to entice customers from one another.

Governments usually fix prices above free market levels
when they wish to change the distribution of income in favour
of producers or owners of the goods. Those producers who actually
manage to sell their goods do benefit, but those producers who are
left with unsold stocks do not. Therefore the overall economic impact
does not conform to the stated aim of the government.

In conclusion, we may restate the consequences of price control. When prices are fixed above or below the free market level then changes occur in the allocation of goods to consumers, the allocation of resources to production and the distribution of income. The actual effects of price controls are often different from their intended effects - a lesson many governments are often slow to learn.

....

Answer 6   **Agricultural Policy**   **Question page 2**
....

Agricultural goods are subject to variations in production for a variety of natural reasons. Excess rainfall, drought, pests and disease occur sporadically to cause differences between the planned output and that actually harvested or produced. Now the demand for foodstuffs is typically inelastic, so that shortages will force up prices considerably and gluts will produce very low prices. If the elasticity of demand is -0.25, for example, then when production falls by 10%, prices rise by 40%. This inherent instability has given rise to a history of government intervention in agricultural markets.

The objectives of such intervention have varied from time to time but two of the most popular advocated have been to stabilize either food prices or farmers' incomes. Assuming the demand curve is relatively stable, price and income fluctuations will be caused by supply fluctuations. A simple way for the government to keep food prices constant would be for them to establish a buffer stock. Then in times of scarcity when the shortage would have caused prices to rise the government releases sufficient stocks to keep the market price constant. In years of bumper crops, when the excess supply would have reduced prices considerably, the government adds to its stocks, again so as to maintain constant market prices.

In Fig. 6, S_1 shows the level of planned output for each market price. D is the relatively inelastic market demand curve. P_1 and Q_1 represent the average market price and quantity sold respectively. When the actual output increases say to Q_2 the government buys $(Q_2 - Q_1)$ to add to its stocks. When output falls below average, say to Q_3 then the government releases $(Q_1 - Q_3)$ to be sold on the market. This policy stabilizes farm

Fig. 6

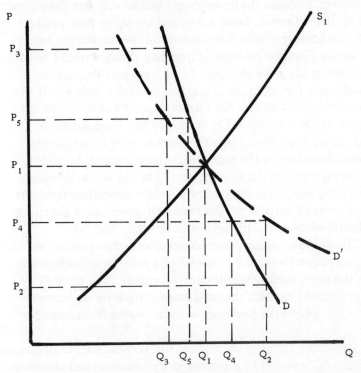

prices completely at P_1 and given this would have been the average equilibrium price, the government can successfully operate this system indefinitely, providing it is prepared to subsidise the scheme to the extent of covering the costs of storage, which are not recovered elsewhere.

The effect of such a price stabilization policy on farmers' income may be seen as follows: whatever the level of current output, the farmers either sell it on the market at price P_1, or the government buys it to add to the buffer stocks, again at a price P_1, i.e. the farmers face a perfectly elastic demand curve at a price P_1. Thus their income which is the total revenue (price times quantity) they earn on the output they sell is directly proportional to the current output level. In poor years their income will be low (as output is low), in good years, their income will be high (as output will be high). Note that this effect on farmers' income is the opposite of what would happen if the government had not intervened.

To turn to the second part of the question. In order to stabilize farmers' incomes the government should stabilize their total revenue. If the farmers faced a demand curve for their product which was unitary elastic then their total revenue would be constant as the effect on revenue of quantity changes would be offset by compensating price changes. As we have said the market demand curve for agricultural goods is typically inelastic. If the government chose to stabilise farmers' income at their average level, i.e. at $TR = P_1Q_1$ in Fig. 6, then when fluctuations in output occur they must allow the market price to vary in the opposite direction by the same percentage amount, by adding or subtracting from their buffer stocks. Thus the actual demand curve facing producers D' is unitary elastic and differs from the market demand curve D by the extent of government purchases or sales (the horizontal difference between D' and D).

To maintain farmers' income constant when production falls to Q_3 we require a price P_5 (since $P_1Q_1 = P_5Q_3$ as both points lie on the same unitary elastic demand curve). At a price P_5, the market demand exceeds the producers' output by an amount $(Q_5 - Q_3)$, which the government must release from its buffer stock.

Stabilizing farmers' incomes in this way reduces fluctuations in prices which would be observed in free markets and also may show an operating surplus. The government would add to its stocks when prices are low, and sell from them when prices are high. If storage costs are not excessive, this scheme will be profitable.

A market economy operates by allowing consumers and producers to come together to negotiate the exchange of goods and services. Firms are assumed to produce in response to effective consumer demands. Given their costs of production and level of technical knowledge the firm, if it maximises profits, will produce at a level of output where marginal costs equals marginal revenue, and marginal cost is rising (or falling less rapidly than marginal revenue if there are increasing returns to scale). The essential point is that firms react to changing conditions of demand, and do not themselves instigate such changes. From this point of view the organisational arrangement of the firm is irrelevant to the smooth operation of the market economy.

This approach may be challenged by considering the influence (through mass media advertising) of large corporations or publicly quoted companies on consumer demand. The growth and development of the modern corporation is due to its advantages over other types of business organisation (better expertise and limited liability) and also the development of a more efficient capital market.

Corporations or joint stock companies are firms incorporated under the companies act 1948. They are separate legal entities from their owners. Almost all are limited companies in the sense that their owners' liability is limited to their investment in the firm. Private companies are usually small and have their stock owned by a few people who generally run the firm. Public companies may issue shares which can be bought by any member of the public, and quoted public companies are those whose shares may be traded on the London Stock Exchange. The dominance of these quoted public companies indicates their relative advantages in raising capital for expansion and spreading risks among large numbers of shareholders.

One important consequence of this dilution of ownership is that the individual shareholders exert little influence on the control of the firm. Management is free, within reasonable limits, to follow its own objectives - perhaps to maximise sales or market share rather than profits. This explains the important role of advertising in the modern corporation, to publicise the product per se, and also to establish product differentiation (real or imaginary).

The development of complex new products requires careful planning and coordination over a long time period. It has been argued that a market economy would never undertake the production of such goods. A large corporation could produce them, however, for with the cooperation of the government (to stabilize the level of economic activity and allow the unbridled expansion of the corporation), and the ability of the corporation to create and sustain demand by mass advertising, marketability is almost certainly guaranteed.

This has led some economists (e.g. J.K. Galbraith) to claim that the competitive market economy is now obsolete and has been replaced by a corporate economy. This is an arguable contention for there are limits to the extent to which demand may be manipulated by advertising. Some new products fail despite enormous advertising campaigns, and some products sell well without any publicity. Shifts in demand are not wholly attributable to advertising campaigns but relate also to the underlying market forces. Secondly the government, through monopoly and environmental legislation, has made some attempts to control the size and output of companies with varying degrees of success.

In conclusion, although at present the modern economy differs substantially from the ideal market economy, it still seems to be some distance from the new industrial state suggested by Galbraith. However we should not discount the possibility that we are at the moment in a transitional phase between the market and corporate system. Only the passage of time will settle the argument.

....

Answer 8   **Sources of Finance**   Question page 3

....

There are four important sources of funds available to firms: undistributed profits, equity, debentures, and bank borrowing. The largest of these is undistributed profits. There are substantial tax advantages in the U.K. to encourage a firm to withhold some of its income rather than pay higher dividends to its shareholders.This income may then be used to finance capital or financial acquisitions.

A second source of finance is the stock exchange. New issues of share capital may be made to obtain funds, but this method is not as important as it once was because government restraints on dividends and taxes on capital gains have reduced the attractiveness of shares to wealth holders.

Debentures and other types of loan stock constitute a third manner of obtaining finance. These are loans, usually of fixed term and rate of interest. Owners of such loan stock are creditors of the firm and must receive payment whether or not profits are being earned.

The residual needs for company finance are generally met by borrowing from banks and other financial institutions. These loans are usually of short duration, but may become long term if the banks agree to their being rolled-over. Many small businesses which are not publicly-quoted rely heavily on this source of finance, which tends to be more expensive than other forms of finance.

To these main four sources may be added government aid of one kind or another (investment grants, temporary employment subsidies). Although these may be important to individual recipient firms, they are not very significant in total.

Let us now consider the impact of an increase in the rate of inflation on the cost of finance from each above source. There are two situations to consider. The inflation may be expected to be either temporary or permanent. If the inflation is expected to persist then all nominal rates of interest will tend to rise by the increase in the rate of inflation. This will raise the costs of new finance from all sources. Bank borrowing and debentures will become more expensive as lenders must be compensated for the higher inflation rate. Issuing new equity will also become more expensive as dividends will have to rise to encourage wealth-holders to acquire additional stocks and shares. The opportunity costs of undistributed profits will also rise as the rate at which the company could have lent out this amount increases. Thus for new capital the relative cost of finance remains unaffected by a permanent rise in the rate of inflation.

A different result emerges, however, when we consider the costs of servicing existing debt. Debentures, being of fixed interest, become relatively cheap to service following a rise in the inflation rate. Since nominal yields and interest rates are pulled up by the rise in the level of inflation, bank borrowing rates, dividends and the opportunity costs of undistributed profits all rise.

Now consider the effect of a temporary rise in the inflation rate. This raises short term rates of interest more than long term rates. Hence bank borrowing and other short term borrowing will become more expensive than longer term loans like debentures. This may only prove temporary for when the inflation abates, short-term rates will fall on bank loans whereas the existing high rate of interest on debentures will be maintained throughout the lifetime of the loan. Similarly the opportunity cost of using undistributed profits will rise temporarily during the period of higher short term nominal rates. Yields on equity will also be pulled upwards but by less than the increase in inflation as they take into account a much longer time period. On existing debts the results are the same except that the fixed interest debenture becomes relatively cheaper compared to other debt where the rate of interest is variable.

Answer 9 **Business Objectives** **Question page 3**

There are two main reasons why firms do not maximise profits. Firstly, they may be unable to pursue this objective because of organisational or informational problems. Secondly they may choose to follow some alternative objectives.

The modern corporation is a complex organisation producing many goods, hence information on economic (as distinct from accounting) costs and revenues associated with producing a specific commodity may be impossible (or very costly) to obtain. So, even if firms want to maximise profits, they may not be in a position to do so, because the required information on marginal cost and marginal revenue is lacking.

In sympathy with this argument, some economists have suggested that entrepreneurs, realising they cannot maximise profits, pursue a full cost pricing policy. This hypothesis states that firms calculate average total costs and add a percentage mark up to determine selling price. Sales are then determined by market demand, thus output, but not price, responds to changes in demand This form of price setting has to a certain extent been institution-alised in the U.K. by the operation of the price code, which only allow price rises if costs have increased.

A second argument against profit maximisation is advocated by some economists who argue that the organisation of a modern corporation affects its output and pricing policy. Decisions are arrived at by compromise between conflicting groups within the firm. This has been developed into a theory of 'satisficing', where firms are assumed to be concerned with achieving maximum values of such target variables as profits or market share, but do not attempt to maximise any single objective. These minimum targets may be achievable over a relatively large range of price and output combinations, so no unique equilibrium is derivable from this theory.

A company is owned by its shareholders, but controlled by its managers. This separation of ownership from control leads to a conflict between the aims of shareholders and the aims of managers. The shareholders would prefer the firm to follow a policy of profit maximisation. The managers are interested in other things: their salaries and power within the company (which is related to the size of the firm and its rate of growth); and perhaps attaining some minimum level of profits or market share sufficient to keep the shareholders content.

One hypothesis which accommodates this behaviour is the sales maximisation theory. Here it is assumed that firms set out to maximise sales revenue, subject to earning a minimum level of profits. Revenue is maximised when marginal revenue is set equal to zero (rather than equal to marginal cost as in the case of the profit maximiser). Assuming the minimum profit constraint is not binding then the sales revenue maximiser will always sell higher output at a lower price than a profit maximiser. This is illustrated in Fig. 7. Given demand and cost conditions, the price that a profit maximiser would set (Ppm) lies above that of a sales maximiser (Psm). Also the profit maximiser's output (Qpm) is less than the sales maximiser's (Qsm).

Fig. 7

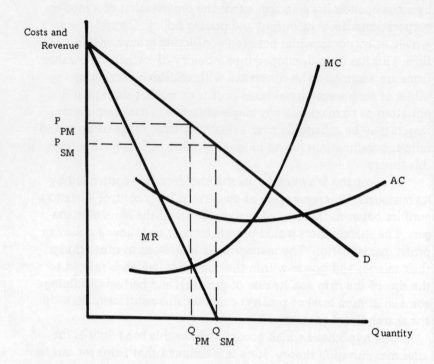

Answer 10   Location of Industry   Question page 3

A profit-maximising firm will decide on the location of a new factory by examining the total costs of production in different regions and choosing that area where costs are minimised. Variations in costs between regions are due to the following factors:

a) availability and costs of raw materials: transportation of bulky or heavy raw materials across wide areas adds dramatically to costs (especially since the oil price rises of recent years). Firms using such raw materials tend to site factories near their supplies.

b) proximity to market: a similar case to the above. Transportation of bulky or heavy finished goods to a far distant market will again raise costs substantially. Firms producing such goods will tend to site close to their markets.

c) regional advantages: costs of production may be affected by climate (important in agriculture). Also, external economies may develop so as to benefit firms moving to the area which are similar or complementary to existing ones. Economies may be due to reduced labour training costs because of the existence of a ready-made pool of skilled labour, and educational facilities for training further skilled workers. Additional external economies may be derivable from marketing considerations eg. a steel producer setting up in Sheffield has the world-wide reputation of Sheffield steel to promote sales.

d) government action: the government provides inducements (e.g. investment grants, capital subsidies) for firms who site production in chosen development areas (and consequently reduce regional unemployment). There are, on the other hand, restrictions on the establishment of new factories in overcrowded industrial connurbations. The size and availability of these financial incentives and physical controls have varied considerably in the past, as consequently have their effectiveness. Sometimes no amount of government assistance will persuade a firm to move away from its source of raw materials, market or external economies.

Answer 11   **Costs**   Question page 3

The short run is defined to be the period during which some factors of production are invariable. These are known as fixed factors and their costs must be met whatever the level of production. Inputs which may be varied with the production level are termed variable factors as the quantities used and therefore costs vary with output. The long run by contrast is the period during which all factors of production may be altered. There are no fixed factors and therefore there are no fixed costs - they do not arise.

In the short run a competitive firm facing a fixed price will offer for sale a quantity determined by its short-run marginal costs. For its short-run supply curve is given by that part of its marginal cost curve above the minimum value of average variable costs. This is shown in Fig. 8, at price P_1, output is given by Q_1. Marginal cost is defined as the increase in total cost resulting from an increase in output of one unit. Since fixed costs do not vary with output, they do not affect marginal costs or average variable costs, and so do not change the position of the supply curve. As far as decisions relating to output are concerned, fixed costs are irrelevant in the short run.

Fig. 8.

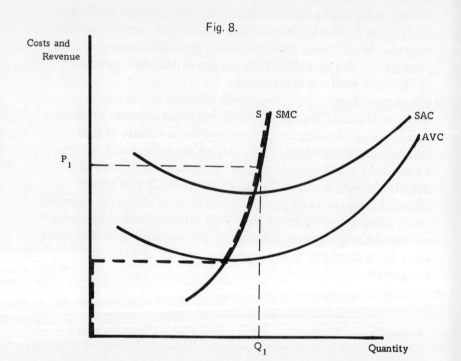

If a competitive firm was in long-run (zero profits) equilibrium then an increase in fixed costs would not affect short-run equilibrium, as we have seen above, but it would have an impact on long-run equilibrium. The increase in costs would create losses and, with freedom of entry and exit, some firms will begin to leave the industry. This will shift the industry supply curve inwards and raise the market price of the product. This pattern will continue until the price rises sufficiently to eliminate losses among the remaining firms. Thus although fixed costs do not arise in the long run, and are irrelevant to the short-run output decision, they do affect the long-run equilibrium of the competitive firm.

The firms optimal factor mix may be determined by a process of cost minimisation. We require the firm to possess information on input productivity and factor and output prices, and how these vary with output.

Consider a firm using several inputs to produce a single good. If we keep all factors except one (A) at a constant level of use, then changes in this variable factor will cause variations in output. The marginal physical product of this input (MPP_A) can be defined as the increase in output generated by using one more unit of this variable factor. From the law of diminishing returns there is a point after which the MPP_A declines with additional increments of the variable factor A.

The value of MPP_A helps to determine the increase in revenue obtained from increased use of factor A. If we assume the product market is competitive then the price at which the firm sells its product is fixed. The increase in revenue generated by selling the additional output, which is known as the marginal revenue product of factor A (MRP_A), is then equal to MPP_A times output price. If the product market is not competitive then the firm faces a downward sloping demand curve. Marginal revenue is less than price and the MRP_A equals MPP_A times marginal revenue.

Increases in the use of factor A reduces the MRP_A, through its effect on MPP_A (due to diminishing returns) and, in non-competitive markets, through the reduced marginal revenue (due to increased sales). Increases in the use of other factors will generally raise the MPP_A and hence MRP_A in competitive markets. In non-competitive markets the increase in MPP_A may be offset by the fall in marginal revenue, so that the total effect on MRP_A is not generally predictable.

The entrepreneur must balance changes in revenue against factor costs. If all factor supplies are perfectly elastic then the firm can buy as much of each input as it wishes at a constant factor cost. Then the ratio of the MRP to factor cost gives the extra revenue obtained by spending an extra pound on this factor. If this ratio varies among different inputs then the entrepreneur can reduce costs by using more of those factors with a high ratio and less of those factors with a low ratio.

The optimal factor mix is obtained when the ratio of MRP to factor price is the same for all inputs.

$$\text{i.e. } \frac{MRP_A}{FP_A} = \frac{MRP_B}{FP_B} = \dots\dots = \frac{MRP_J}{FP_J}$$

where MRP = Marginal revenue product
FP = factor price,
and A,B, ... J are inputs

So the value of an extra pound spent on each input is the same. Only when this condition is met will costs be minimised, and the optional factor mix determined.

Answer 13   **Returns to Scale/Factor**   **Question page 4**

Returns to scale and returns to a factor are both concerned with changes in output caused by varying the level of inputs. However, the concept of returns to scale involves the effect on output of variations in all inputs simultaneously in the same proportions. whereas returns to a factor looks at the effect of output of changes in one variable input holding others at a constant level.

Consider the effect of raising all input quantities by a fixed percentage x%. If output rises by more than x% then there are said to be increasing returns to scale. If output rises by exactly x%, then there are constant returns to scale. Should output rise by less than x% then decreasing returns to scale are indicated. The type of returns to scale can be used to explain the shape of the long-run cost curve of a firm [1].

a) increasing returns: as output rises faster than costs, long-run average cost (LAC) is falling, and long-run marginal cost (LMC) lies below LAC.

b) constant returns: output and costs rise at the same rate and LAC equals LMC which is constant.

c) decreasing returns: output is rising at a slower rate than costs, so LAC is rising and LMC lies above LAC.

It is possible for a firm to exhibit varying returns to scale over its feasible range of output, and this is shown in Fig. 9.

---

[1] To simplify, assume factor supplies are perfectly elastic, so that costs rise proportionately to factor use.

Returns to factor relates to the change in the marginal physical product of a variable factor as its use increases and all other inputs are held constant. The marginal physical product is the increase in output generated by employing an additional unit of the factor. Empirical observation has led to the formulation of a law of diminishing returns to scale. This states that there is some level of factor use after which subsequent increments of the input lead to declines in the marginal physical product.

The law of diminishing returns has implications for the short-run cost curves of the firm. It follows from the law that each unit of input costs the same amount but adds less and less to output (eventually). Accordingly, to increase output by one unit at a time, we require ever larger increments of the factor. Therefore short-run average costs (SAC) eventually slope upwards, and short-run marginal costs (SMC) eventually lie above SAC.[1]

Fig. 9

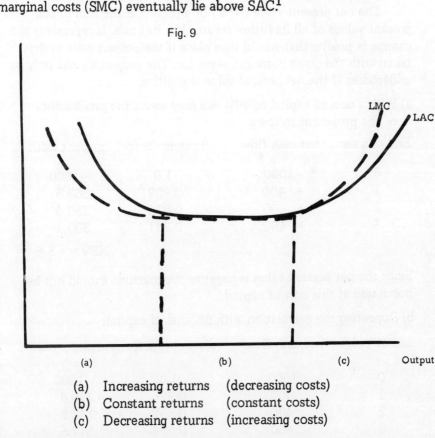

(a)   Increasing returns   (decreasing costs)
(b)   Constant returns   (constant costs)
(c)   Decreasing returns   (increasing costs)

[1] e.g. see Fig. 8 on page 38 for an illustration of this.

In order to compare the value of the returns from the project with the cost we have to use the method of discounting. This involves finding the present value of sums of money payable at different times in the future. The present value (PV) of £x payable in n years time, with the rate of interest r, is given by the formula:

$$PV = \frac{£x}{(1+r)^n}$$

The term $\frac{1}{(1+r)^n}$ is the discount factor given in the table beneath the question. Therefore the present value is equal to the future sum multiplied by the appropriate discount factor.

The net present value (NPV) of a project is the sum of the present values of all its future returns less its costs. It represents the change in profits that would take place if the project were undertaken with the given costs and revenues. The project should only be undertaken if the net present value is positive.

a) With a cost of capital of 10%, we may assess the profitability of the project as follows:

End of year	net cash flow	discount factor	present value
0	−1000	1.0	−1000
1	+ 400	0.909	363.6
2	+ 400	0.826	330.4
3	+ 400	0.751	300.4
			NPV = −5.6

Since the net present value is negative the machine should not be purchased at this cost of capital.

b) Repeating the calculation with 8% cost of capital.

End of year	net cash flow	discount factor	present value
0	−1000	1.0	−1000
1	400	0.926	370.4
2	400	0.857	342.8
3	400	0.794	317.6
			NPV = 30.8

Since the NPV is now positive the machine should be purchased.

Perfect competition is characterised by a large number of firms producing an identical product. Each firm is a price taker, and this price is set where market demand equals supply. There is freedom of entry and exit, and firms have perfect knowledge of all relevant economic and technical information.

Under this highly stylised set of conditions long-run equilibrium is obtained when price equals marginal cost (short-run and long-run) and excess profits are zero. The marginal cost curve is the firm's supply curve (above the minimum level of average variable cost). The addition of each firm's supply gives the market supply at any given price.

Imposing a lump-sum tax (T) raises fixed costs by the amount of the tax. Average costs increase by T/q but marginal costs are unchanged. Supply is not affected in the short-run, price and quantity remain constant and temporary losses are endured.

In the long-run firms will leave this loss-making industry. This will shift the market supply curve inwards and consequently raise the price. Those firms remaining in the industry will gradually make smaller losses and eventually these will vanish. This is shown in Fig. 10. The left-hand diagram shows the industry supply (S) and demand (D) curves. The equilibrium price is P_1 which, from the right-hand diagram, is seen to yield zero profits. When the lump-sum tax is imposed long-run average costs (LAC) move up to LAC'. As firms leave the industry the industry supply curve shifts to S', market price rises from P_1 to P_2 (by less than T/q) and aggregate output falls from Q_1 to Q_2. Long-run equilibrium is therefore restored with a smaller number of firms each producing a higher output (q_2 rather than q_1).

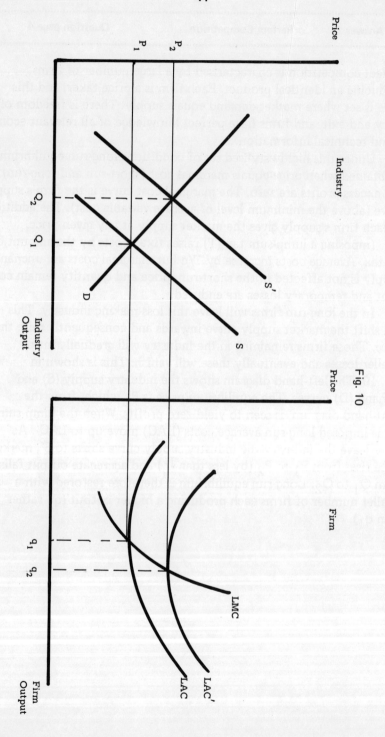

Fig. 10

The level of advertising expenditure undertaken by a firm depends both on the cost of alternative forms of advertising and on the alternative revenue so generated. The relative costs of advertising are almost equal among firms, although there are sometimes economies of scale reflecting discounts for a minimum run of advertisements. The extra revenue generated by advertising depends critically on the type of market environment facing the firm.

In a perfectly competitive market structure the firm faces a horizontal demand curve. It will not pay such a firm to advertise its product, since it can already sell as much as it wishes at the current given market price. Thus advertising would add to costs but not to revenue.

A monopolist may undertake advertising to promote his product if the additional marginal revenue obtained by manipulating the demand curve in this way outweighs his advertising costs. To maximise profits he should increase his level of advertising until the marginal cost of advertising equals the marginal revenue from increased sales.

The majority of firms are in neither of the above extreme market situations. They operate in the range between under various conditions of imperfect competition: the two main categories are monopolistic competition and oligopoly. The impact and nature of advertising expenditure can be expected to be fundamentally different in each case.

The monopolistically competitive firm is one of many producing a similar good (but not identical) to his competitors. He faces a downward sloping demand curve, and in the short-run behaves like a monopolist. The role of advertising in this environment is to establish product differentiation and increase demand. If this is successful, the firm earns excess profits. In the long-run there is freedom of entry into the industry. High profit levels will therefore attract new firms into the production of similar goods. This reduces each firm's share of the overall market, and consequently shifts their demand curve to the left. In the long run the excess profits are eliminated and the firm breaks even. The firm is forced to keep its advertising expenditure to maintain its market share and avoid bankruptcy.

An oligopoly consists of a few large firms producing similar goods. Each firm realises that the demand for its product is influenced by the prices charged by all firms in the industry. This may lead to a tacit agreement among firms not to compete by undercutting rivals' prices in case a price-war is initiated. Such price stickiness is a prediction of several theories of oligopoly behaviour. Firms must then compete for market share in other ways, such as expensive advertising campaigns. This advertising will usually be brand- not product-orientated, and concerned with improving market share rather than market size.

Oligopolistic firms may also use advertising as a barrier to entry where there are few economies of scale. If the minimum efficient scale of production (MES) were relatively small compared to total demand then new entrants could enter the industry relatively easily. If existing firms are advertising heavily to promote the brand image, then so will new entrants. Adding the advertising costs to the production costs shifts the shape and position of the average total cost curve, increasing the MES and thus making it more difficult for new firms to enter the industry. This is illustrated in **Fig. 11**, where the MES has been shifted from MES_1 to MES_2 by the high level of advertising.

Fig. 11

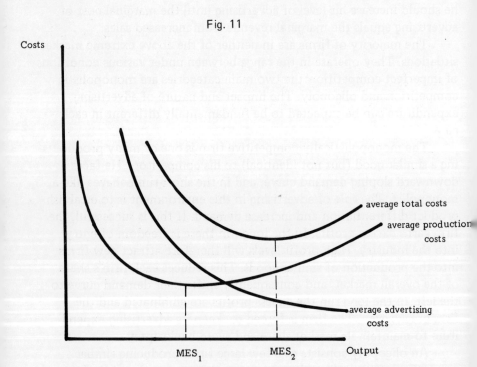

From the given information it is necessary to calculate the values of total revenue, marginal revenue, marginal cost and average cost.

Price £	Output (units)	Total revenue £	Marginal revenue £	Total cost £	Marginal cost £	Average cost £
10	10	100	8	170	2	17.00
9	20	180	6	190	2.5	9.50
8	30	240	4	215	3.5	7.01
7	40	280	2	250	5.0	6.25
6	50	300	0	300	7.0	6.00
5	60	300	-	370	-	6.17

i) A profit - maximising monopolist will increase output while this adds more to revenue than costs. By inspecting the marginal cost and marginal revenue tables we see that an output level of 30, marginal revenue (£40) exceeds marginal cost (£35) and it will pay him to produce an extra 10 units. At an output of 40 marginal revenue (£20) is less than marginal cost (£10), so it will not pay him to expand production beyond this point. Thus the profit - maximising output level is 40 and the price is £7.

ii) The price elasticity of demand is defined as:

$$E = \frac{\text{Percentage change in quantity demanded}}{\text{Percentage change in price}}$$

Consider the effect of a price fall from 7 to 6. The percentage change is $-\frac{1}{7} \times 100\%$. From the demand schedule quantity will rise from 40 to 50, a percentage change of $\frac{10}{40} = \frac{1}{4} \times 100\%$

Therefore

$$E = \frac{\frac{1}{4} \times 100\%}{-\frac{1}{7} \times 100\%} = -1\frac{3}{4}$$

iii) By inspection, price and average cost are equal at an output level of 50 units.

iv) The major reasons why a monopoly is considered evil are a) it charges a higher price and offers a lower quantity for sale as compared to competitive firms, and b) it operates less efficiently. These criticisms of monopoly assume there are no economies of scale, so that costs are identical and comparisons may be made between the different prices and quantities obtained from the monopoly and competitive market situations. We may use the example to illustrate these points.

If the firm were run as a competitive industry then output would be 50 units, as given under part (iii) and price £6. The firm would be producing at minimum average cost (also £6) and therefore efficiently. The monopolist from part (i) charges a higher price £7, sells a lower quantity 40, and produces them at a higher average cost £6.25 (and therefore less efficiently). These results justify the criticisms of monopoly, given our assumption of no economies of scale.

....

Answer 18   Price Discrimination   Question page 5
....

A price discriminating monopolist is one who charges different prices (not reflected by variations in cost) to different customers. This is only feasible when some customers are prepared to pay more for the good than others and resale of the good is impossible.

The limiting form of perfect price discrimination occurs when the monopolist is able to charge each buyer the maximum he is prepared to pay. In this case the demand curve is also the marginal revenue curve and the profit-maximising level of output is given by the intersection of the marginal cost curve with demand. This is shown at Q_2 in Fig. 12. A uniform pricing monopolist would produce at Q_1, where his marginal revenue and marginal cost intersect, and charge P_1. The additional profit earned by the policy of discrimination can be determined by analysing the differences in revenue and costs in the two cases. The discriminating monopolist's revenue exceeds that of the uniform pricer's by the areas of AP_1B plus BEQ_2Q_1. His costs only rise by CEQ_2Q_1. Thus his resulting extra profit is the sum of areas AP_1B plus BCE (shaded on the diagram).

Fig. 12

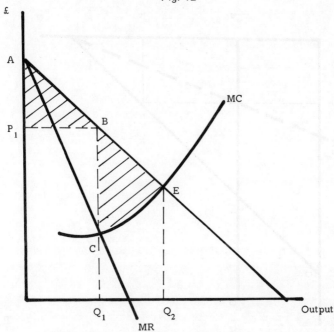

Another common form of discrimination occurs when a monopolist sells in two distinct markets e.g. home and abroad. Discrimination will be possible if the price elasticities of demand differ in the
two markets. For simplicity assume he is a monopolist in the home
market and sells abroad under conditions of perfect competition.
If marginal costs of production are the same whichever market is
supplied then the discriminating monopolist will maximise profits
by setting marginal revenues in the two markets equal to marginal
cost (MC). On the left hand diagram in Fig. 13, D_1 and MR_1 are the
home market demand and marginal revenue curves. $D_2 = MR_2$ cor-
responds to those of the export market. By horizontal addition we
can find both the aggregate demand (D^*) and marginal revenue
(MR^*) drawn on the right-hand diagram in Fig. 13. The intersection
of MC with MR^* determines total output (Q), and the allocation to
the home market can be read from MR_1 to be Q_1. The amount
exported Q_2 is $Q - Q_1$. The prices charged in each market are given
by the respective demand curves as P_1 and P_2.

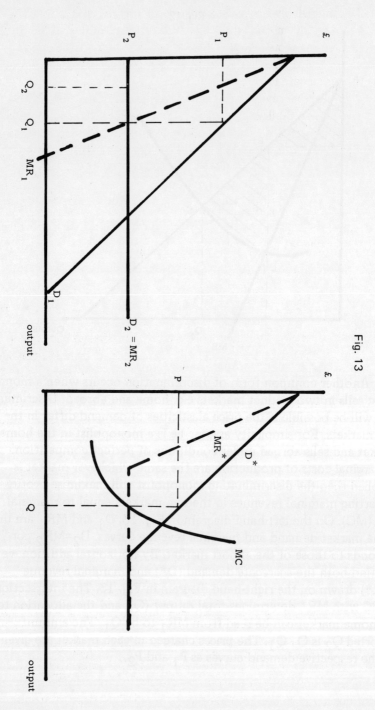

Fig. 13

A monopolist who chose not to discriminate would again set MR* equal to MC and produce the same total output Q. The price he would charge would be obtained from the aggregage demand curve D at P_3 in Fig. 13. This is above the competitive price P_2 in the export market. Thus he would only sell in the home market. Since the marginal revenue in the home market is less than in the export market, a reallocation of part of the output from home to export would increase revenue while costs are unchanged. Therefore the discriminating monopolist would earn higher profits.

Answer 19   **Restrictive Practices**   Question page 6

There are two alternative approaches which governments could follow in formulating policy towards monopolies and restrictive practices. The structural approach would argue that the existence of a monopoly or restrictive practice is undesirable per se. The assumptions are that monopolists will always misallocate resources and restrictive trade practices always act against the interests of the consumer. Therefore both should either be banned or made the subject of government investigation. The second line of reasoning is derived from the behavioral approach, which stresses the importance of the effects of the monopoly or trade practice on the public interest, rather than their mere existence. This suggests the government should only act against individual monopolies or practices which abuse this public interest.

With the passing in 1948 of the Monopolies and Restrictive Practices Act the U.K. government chose the behavioural view. The Monopolies and Restrictive Practices Commission was established to investigate and report on cases referred to it by various government departments. Its brief was to defend the public interest, but this concept was to some extent ambiguous. A monopoly was defined to exist when at least one third of the total output was supplied by a single firm (or group). This was rather arbitrary for the extent of monopoly power depends crucially on the size and existence of competitors. The 1973 Fair Trading Act, in recognising this, reduced the relevant market share to 25%. A number of monopolists were investigated and cleared by the commission (e.g. I.C.I. - chemical fertilizers) of behaviour contrary to the public interest. Even in those cases where the monopoly commission found a firm had abused its monopoly position the recommendations were often overruled by the Board of Trade (e.g. Imperial Tobacco).

However, a large number of restrictive practices were investigated and reported by the Commission. Nearly always they were found to be against the public interest. They tended to involve price fixing or agreeing market shares between firms to bolster profits at the expense of the consumer. Legislation in 1956 (Restrictive Practices Act) tightened the controls on trade practices to such an extent that we may conclude that with respect to these practices the behavioural approach has been dropped and a structural view adopted. Only in exceptional circumstances may a restrictive practice be permitted, and even then it has to be registered with the Restrictive Practices Court.

Monopoly and merger policy has continued to be based on the behavioural view. The onus is on the Monopoly Commission to show that a monopoly (or potential monopoly in the case of a merger) acts against the public interest. In 1965 the Monopoly and Merger Act was passed empowering the government to stop a merger, but it was still required to prove its case against the monopoly.

This difference in emphasis between monopoly legislation and restrictive practices arises because the economic argument against monopolies is not clear cut. On grounds of allocative efficiency, it is true that monopolists do not operate at the minimum average cost level, and set prices above marginal costs. But if there are substantial production economies of scale this monopoly price may still be lower than that charged in a highly - competitive industry composed of small firms operating well below the minimum efficient scale of production. This is shown in Fig. 14. Given the demand and marginal revenues curves D & MR, a monopolist facing a marginal cost curve MC will produce at Q_M where MR = MC and charge a price P_M. If the monopoly were broken up into much smaller units then costs could rise so that the industry supply curve under competitive conditions is given by S. Hence the competitive equilibrium price and quantity would be given by P_c and Q_c respectively. Note that if economies of scale are due solely to excessive advertising expenditure then this constitutes an effective barrier to entry, and is an argument against the monopoly.[1]

It is also often claimed that substantial economies of scale are obtained on research and development (R & D) expenditure. This would suggest that large firms can reduce their costs faster than small firms, as they introduce better products or more productive methods more quickly.

[1] See the answer to Q.16 for elaboration on this point.

Fig. 14

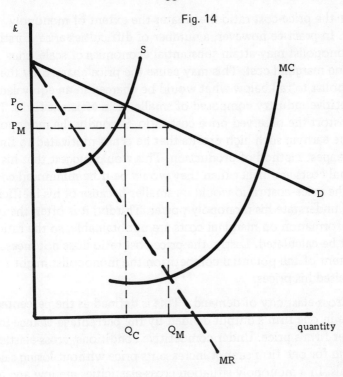

Answer 20   Economic Concentration   Question page 6

Pure monopoly is a rare phenomenon in private industry in
that a single firm producing a good with no close substitutes and
therefore no competitors is seldom observed. More often we find a
dominant firm in an industry in which other perhaps smaller firms
produce similar products. Measuring the extent of the monopoly
power of the dominant firm in such cases is not easy. A number of
alternative methods have been suggested and used but they are all
subject to various criticisms.
a)   The price-cost ratio: This measure is defined as the difference
between price and marginal cost divided by price. Under long-run
competitive equilibrium price equals marginal cost, and so this
measure would give a value of zero, indicating (correctly) an absence
of monopoly power. Under monopoly, price is set above marginal
cost and so the ratio would give a positive value. Accordingly, the

greater the price-cost ratio the greater the extent of monopoly power. In practice however, a number of difficulties arise. Firstly the monopolist may attain substantial economies of scale, thus reducing marginal cost. This may cause the price charged by the monopolist to fall below what would be charged in an equivalent competitive industry composed of smaller, less-efficient firms. This may distort the observed price-cost ratio. Secondly the monopolist may be earning such high profits that he is not motivated to find the cheapest method of production. This would suggest that his marginal costs are higher than they would be if he minimised costs. Thus the price-cost ratio would be smaller because of his inefficiency and so understate his monopoly power. Thirdly, it is often the case that information on marginal costs are unobtainable, so the ratio cannot be calculated. Lastly, the price-cost ratio does not measure the extent of the potential competition the monopolist might face if he raised his prices.

b)   Cross-elasticity of demand: This is defined as the percentage change in one firm's output divided by the percentage change in another firm's price. Under competitive conditions, cross-elasticities are high for one firm cannot increase its price without losing sales to its rivals. In a monopoly situation cross-elasticities are low and a firm may raise its price without significant loss of sales. The lower the cross-elasticity of demand, the greater the level of monopoly power. The main criticism of this measure results from its attempted use in imperfect markets, such as oligopoly. Here firms realise that competitors may respond to price changes by altering their own prices or advertising to maintain market share. This may completely swamp the cross-elasticity effect.

c)   Excess Profits: It is claimed that the greater the monopoly power of a firm the larger its excess profits will be. But, although it is true that a competitive firm in the long-run equilibrium earns no excess profits,it is not the case that excess profits indicate monopoly power or that a monopolist always earns excess profits. Firstly the monopoly may be operating in a high cost industry, where even he can only just cover costs. Secondly, as under a) the monopolist may be operating inefficiently and so earn no profits. Also, excess profits may be the result of short-run shifts in demand, or innovation by competitive firms, rather than monopoly power.

d)   N - Firm Concentration ratios: These are a measure of the proportion of output (or employment, or some other variable indicating relative size) provided by the N largest firms in a particular industry.

They are the most widely used method of estimating monopoly power. Under competitive conditions a single firm's output is negligible compared with the total so that for example the 3-firm concentration ratio is close to zero. A pure monopoly would give a one firm concentration ratio of 100%. For a given number of firms a high concentration ratio denotes a great extent of monopoly power. Again this method has its disadvantages. Firstly, under conditions of imperfect competition and differentiated products it is often extremely difficult to draw a boundary where one industry ends and another begins. Secondly changes in the relative importance of the N largest firms may .not be related to the extent of the monopoly power wielded by any one firm. Finally there may be some understatement of the extent of monopoly power exerted by a firm if it operates in several separate but related markets.

Answer 21   **Nationalized Industries**   **Question page 6**

The meaning of the opening quotation is ambiguous until "true costs" are defined. It is not clear whether this term refers to marginal or average costs, or if it included all social costs or just private costs.

Marginal-cost pricing requires the consumer to pay a price equal to the costs of production of the last marginal unit of the commodity. To the extent that this represents the opportunity costs of production then such a pricing policy will lead to increased efficiency. However, there are some problems associated with this. Firstly if economies of scale are prevalent in the industry then marginal costs are less than average costs. Therefore marginal cost pricing will lead to inevitable losses. How should these be financed? If extra taxes are raised to meet the losses then this implies a redistribution of income will occur to those users of the commodity from tax payers. Alternatively a two-part tariff system may be introduced where consumers pay a fixed amount (sufficient to cover the loss) plus a variable amount equal to marginal cost. This system has been adopted by various Nationalised Industries in the U.K. (gas, electricity, telephones).

Average-cost pricing results in zero-profits (provided the demand curve does not lie everywhere below average costs). Consequently there is no problem involved in financing an industry which adopts this policy, providing all the economic costs are included. If there are economies of scale then average-cost pricing

will result in a higher price (P_2) and a smaller output (Q_2) than
marginal - cost pricing (P_1 and Q_1), as shown in Fig. 15. Also,
the average-cost prices will be producing less efficiently than the
marginal - cost prices, since the latter generally produces at a lower
level of average costs.

The distinction between private and social costs is important
for the operation of a pricing policy. Private costs measure the
opportunity cost of resources paid for by the firm. Social costs
measure the opportunity cost of all resources used by the firm
whether they are paid for by the firm (private costs) or other
members of society (external costs). A divergence between private
and social cost indicates that the firm is using resources which it
regards as costless, but which society regards as having positive
value. It is argued that Nationalised industries should base their
pricing policy on social rather than private costs, reflecting the
'national interest'. However this policy is often not feasible
because of an inability to quantify the full social costs. In such
cases the pricing policy adopted may be fairly arbitrary.

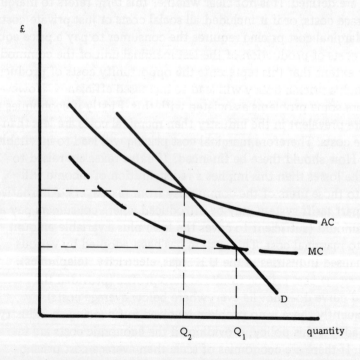

Fig. 15

The problem of determining marginal social costs may be confounded by the existence of joint products. For example if a small branch railway is an important feeder to a main line, then the marginal costs of providing either service are interrelated. Which costs should be considered in the formulation of the pricing policy in such cases is often difficult or impossible to determine.

In a competitive market structure, firms are forced to minimise costs just to stay in business. Short-term profits may be earned, but eventually the entrance of new firms attracted by these profits will reduce revenue until it only just covers long-run costs. In a nationalised industry there is no such competitive pressure to minimise costs. This may lead to inefficiency and reduce productivity. In such a situation no pricing policy can be optimal. If the consumer pays the true cost of the goods, the nationalised industry should at least ensure that this cost is minimised.

....

Answer 22   **Industrial Structure**   **Question page 6**

....

Under certain conditions the market mechanism provides an efficient method of allocating resources to the production of goods and services. Changes in relative prices, which occur in response to variations in demand and supply, alter the average profit-rate in each industry. Over time new firms are attracted to the more profitable markets and existing firms leave those where losses are made. Thus a restructuring of the economy takes place which maintains economic efficiency.

Critics of this line of reasoning argue that the assumptions required for a market economy to achieve and maintain economic efficiency over time are not met in practice. Divergences between private and social costs, market imperfections (factor immobility, lack of information about products, or non-optimising behaviour by firms), and the existence of collective goods require a government to intervene in the market if economic efficiency is to be achieved.

Until fairly recently government intervention in the U.K. has not been dominated by this motive of efficiency. Often policy was determined by such macro-economic considerations as the level of unemployment or the balance of payments. Loss-making firms such as British Leyland, have been supported by government money partly to avoid higher imports and partly to avoid redundancies on a very large scale. Such government intervention did little to reverse the relative decline of British Industry in world markets. One reason for this relative decline may be a change in the distribution of the British labour force that took place in the period from 1961-1976. There has been a shift away from employment in the manufacturing sector towards the service sector (especially public services). This makes it difficult for manufacturing industry to expand when facing increased demand because of labour shortages. In addition the growth of the public sector has used up physical resources, which has created further obstacles in the path of industrial reorganisation and expansion.

In 1975 The British Government announced a new approach to Industrial strategy. This new strategy was based on a commitment to increased efficiency, productivity and growth. Several sector working parties were set up to examine how individual industries could be helped by government action. The Industry Act established the National Enterprise Board as a publicly owned holding company. In addition to several assets acquired earlier, the government provided the N.E.B. with a financial provision to expand its influence in the manufacturing sector. Its main objectives were to i) earn a commercially acceptable return on its assets (15−20% by 1981), ii) stimulate productive capacity in important areas (by providing risk capital), iii) reduce regional differences in unemployment rates by positive discrimination when alternative sites for new production were available, iv) improve the efficiency and capacity of export industries and v) establish and support domestic industries which produce alternatives to imported goods.

It may be argued that if a company is able to provide a commercial return, then any finance it required for expansion could be obtained from existing financial institutions. Only high-risk or loss-making companies could not raise the necessary cash by this method, and these are the type of companies the N.E.B. have assisted.

At the present time the N.E.B. is failing to meet many of its stated objectives. Firstly in its second annual report (May 1978) it lists a loss of £31 million (mainly due to Leyland's losses). Secondly, those companies which received assistance have generally reduced their manpower in the drive for increased productivity thus increasing unemployment rates. Little progress has been achieved on stimulating import substitutes or creating new industries. Some progress has been made in raising the levels of investment (and hence capacity) in assisted firms. Whether this will succeed in reversing the decline in British industry is unlikely without complementary action to free resources from other sectors of the economy.

....

Answer 23 **Marginal Productivity Theory** Question page 7

....

A profit maximising firm will hire inputs until the extra revenue generated from the last unit employed equals the factor cost. This extra revenue generated is known as the marginal revenue product (MRP), which is the product of marginal physical product (MPP) and marginal revenue (MR). The MPP is the additional output produced by hiring one more unit of the factor. Marginal revenue is the increase in revenue obtained by selling an extra unit of output. From the law of diminishing returns the MPP declines as additional units of the factor are employed. If the firm sells in a competitive market then MR is constant If, on the other hand, it sells in an imperfect market then MR falls as the firm has to reduce price to sell a greater quantity.

Thus as factor use increases the MRP falls. For a given factor cost the firm will hire units of that factor until the additional revenue contributed by the last unit (MRP) is equal to its cost. So the firm's demand for a factor of production is given by its MRP curve.

The elasticity of demand for a factor of production is defined as the percentage change in quantity demanded divided by the percentage change in factor price. This elasticity is related to changes in both MPP and MR. How the MPP varies as additional units of factor are employed is important, for if diminishing returns set in very quickly then the MPP will fall rapidly as more units of the factor are employed. In this case, even if the factor price fell considerably, there would be little incentive to purchase many extra units of the factor as they would contribute very little additional output and consequently the elasticity of demand for the factor would be low.

Secondly, if marginal revenue falls relatively quickly as output rises, then there will be little incentive to increase factor use following a fall in its price. The value of marginal revenue depends on the elasticity of demand in the output market. In competitive markets this elasticity is infinite and MP is constant, equal to the going price of output. For a given MPP the maximum value for MRP is given by P.MPP. For less than infinite elasticity, MR falls as output rises, and the value of marginal revenue product declines steadily as the elasticity diminishes until it reaches zero when the demand curve is unitary elastic.

Two further factors offset price elasticity of an input: the degree with which factors are substitutable and the percentage of total costs accounted for by a particular factor. If a firm can substitute one factor for another relatively easily following a rise in factor price then the price elasticity will be high. Also, if a factor does not contribute significantly to total costs then a rise in its price will not have a large effect on costs, prices and therefore output. Its elasticity will therefore be relatively low.

Answer 24 **Factor Mobility** Question page 7

In deciding where to produce firms must take account of the cost and availability of factors and raw materials, and the transport costs of supplying markets with their output. If there is a relatively cheap and plentiful supply of labour in one area this may not be enough to attract firms if it is too far from their markets, or raw materials are not available. Unless labour can move to where there is a demand for its services unemployment will rise and/or wages will fall in this area relative to the national averages. Immobility of labour, then, is one reason for the differences in regional unemployment levels.

When shifts in the pattern of demand occur, the prices of products and factors vary to alter the returns available to each factor in its different uses. All factors (land, labour and capital) may be slow to respond to these market forces. Such immobility may be seen as a failure to move from one area to another (geographical immobility) or from one use to another (occupational immobility). Land is geographically very immobile and, once built upon, may also be immobile in use. Capital mobility between alternative uses depends on the degree of specialization of particular equipment. The more specific the use the less mobile the capital equipment will be. For example office equipment is much more mobile than a textile loom. The geographical mobility of much capital is often very low due to the high costs of dismantling and moving it elsewhere.

The mobility of labour between occupations depends on whether the specific skills associated with alternative forms of employment and the skills acquired from education, training or job experience by the labour force can be matched. The more highly specialised the occupation, the less mobile will be the labour force in responce to market changes. The lack of geographical mobility exhibited by the labour force in the U.K. has contributed to regional problems of unemployment. Workers may be relatively tied to their jobs for a number of reasons: lack of knowledge or uncertainty about job prospects elsewhere, strong social ties with the local community and firm, or potential loss of seniority or pension rights.

Regional variations in unemployment may also be attributable to a failure of labour markets to allocate resources properly. In some areas an excess supply of labour may become a regular feature if the wage rate is fixed at too high a level. This rigidity of wages may be caused by collective bargaining on a national scale, and would reduce labour mobility by failing to provide a financial incentive to change occupation or move elsewhere. If there are non-monetary advantages (cheap housing, good leisure facilities, etc.) to offset the poor employment opportunities then workers may prefer not to move to other areas, especially if unemployment benefit cushions some of the financial hardship of being out of work. This too will reduce labour mobility.

If the costs of transporting raw materials and finished goods were not significant and if capital were perfectly mobile then firms could be attracted to areas of cheap and plentiful labour, and so reduce the level of unemployment. If labour were perfectly mobile, then it could move elsewhere to obtain employment, providing the training and educational facilities were sufficient for then to acquire the relevant skills. Therefore it is the immobility of both labour and capital which contribute to the regional variations in unemployment.

Trade unions are associations of workers which negotiate collectively with employers to improve pay and general working conditions. In a particular industry a trade union may succeed in obtaining a higher wage than would have been offered without collective bargaining. However, if the demand curve for labour is not perfectly inelastic this higher wage will cause a fall in employment. This is shown in Fig. 16. The intersection of the demand curve D and supply curve S gives the pre-union wage W_1 and amount of labour sold L_1. After the union has negotiated a higher wage W_2 employment falls to L_2 and there is an excess supply of labour equal to $(L_3 - L_2)$. Those workers made redundant and new workers attracted by the higher wage will exert downward pressure on the wage rate. If the union is to be able to sustain W_2 it must restrict the supply of labour.

Such control may be achieved by stipulating minimum requirements (in terms of education and/or training, etc.) and operating a closed shop. This will shift the supply curve inwards, say to S′ in the diagram, and hence establish W_2 as the new equilibrium wage.

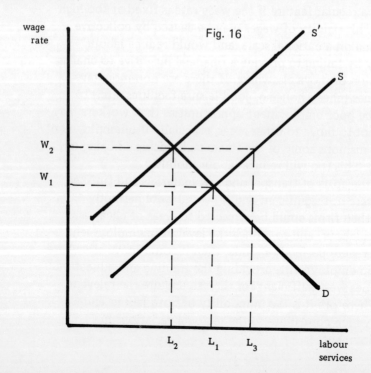

Fig. 16

In certain circumstances the union may be able to increase wages in a particular industry without generating unemployment. Firstly, if the firm is making large profits in highly imperfect markets it may be more willing to give in to large pay claims than risk the possibility of an expensive strike action. This would transfer some of the excess profits from firms to workers. Even if profits are not high the firm may consider the opportunity cost of a strike to be much greater than the cost of aggreeing higher wages, especially if the union has substantial financial resources to support striking members and if the firm's fixed costs are relatively higher than its labour costs.

A second situation where unions can achieve higher wages without lower employment is when the firm is a monopsonist (i.e. sole buyer) in the local labour market. This is shown in Fig. 17. Again the firm's demand for labour is given by D and the supply of labour is S. This supply curve represents the employer's average cost of labour (wage per employer). The firm, being a monopsonist, is aware that if it wishes to hire more labour it must pay

Fig. 17

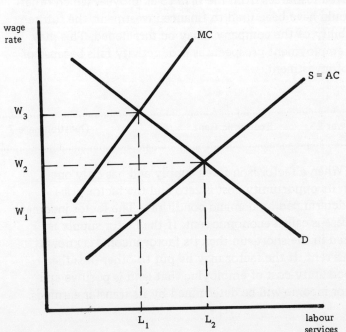

a higher wage, not just to the extra workers, but to all employers. So the marginal cost (MC) to the firm of hiring additional labour is greater than the average cost, and so the MC curve lies above the AC curve in Fig. 17. If the firm equates marginal cost with marginal revenue product (its demand curve) it will employ fewer workers (L_1) and can reduce wages to W_1.

A union in such a situation may be in a position to increase both wages and employment. Suppose a wage rate W_2 is negotiated. Then up to an employment level L_2 the firm must pay each worker the same wage W_2. Effectively, W_2 replaces the firm's marginal and average costs curves for labour over the relevant range of employment. Again the union is faced with a choice between wages and employment. As the negotiated wage increases between W_1 and W_2, so employment rises from L_1 to L_2. As the wage rises from W_2 to W_3 employment falls back from L_2 to L_1.

In the long-run an increase in wages lowers the relative price of capital. This may induce the firm to use a more capital intensive production method. If so, the demand curve for labour may shift inwards putting downward pressure on wages and employment. In addition if higher wages have transferred resources from the firm to employees which otherwise would have been used to finance investment, the future profitability of the company may be threatened. This may reduce employment prospects as productivity falls because of a lack of investment.

Answer 26   **Economic Rent**   Question page 7

When a factor is in fixed supply and has only one use then its opportunity cost is zero and the factor price will be determined by demand conditions. The factor income in this case is called economic rent. If the factor supply is only fixed in the short-run then its factor income is known as a quasi-rent. If the factor may be put to other uses then the opportunity cost of employing that land is positive and the factor income will be determined by its transfer earnings.

In the short-run, the total supply of land available for use as cinema seats is fixed. If the relationship between land and cinema seats is constant (e.g. 1 sq. metre of land has to be used to provide 1 cinema seat) then the supply of cinema seats will be fixed. The opportunity cost of the land is, therefore, zero and the price of cinema seats (and the land used by them) will be determined by the demand for cinema seats. The factor income is a quasi-rent as the supply is temporarily fixed. The first statement is therefore a correct interpretation of the short-run market situation.

In the long-run, the price of land available for use as cinema seats depends on its opportunity cost, i.e. the income it could obtain if used elsewhere. The supply of land for cinema seats in the long-run is perfectly elastic at its going transfer price. The demand for land to be used in creating cinema seats will therefore only determine the quantity of land used and not its price. Given the constant relationship between land and cinema seats then the supply of cinema seats will also be perfectly elastic. Hence the demand for cinema seats will determine quantity but not price. The price of cinema seats will be determined by the transfer price of land. If the price of land rises then in the long-run the price of cinema seats will be high. Thus the second statement is true in the long-run.

The following diagrams depict factor and output markets in the short-run and long-run. The market situations given in Figs. 18 (a) and (b) illustrate the short-run with inelastic supply of land (S_L) and cinema seats (S_{CS}), and downward sloping demand curves for land (D_L) and cinema seats (D_{CS}). In both markets price is determined by demand. In Figs. 18 (c) and (d) the same demand curves are given, but because land is now in perfectly elastic supply (S_L) at its given transfer price (P_L), the supply of cinema seats (S_{CS}) is also perfectly elastic at a constant price (P_{CS}). P_{CS} is determined by the price of land (P_L) multiplied by the amount of land required to produce one cinema seat (ignoring other costs). Both above statements are therefore correct but they apply to different time periods.

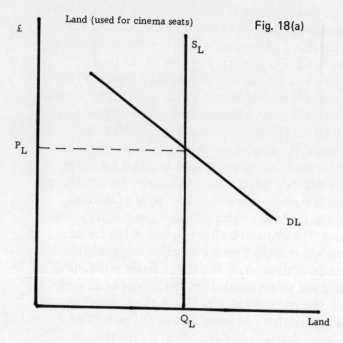

Land (used for cinema seats)   Fig. 18(a)

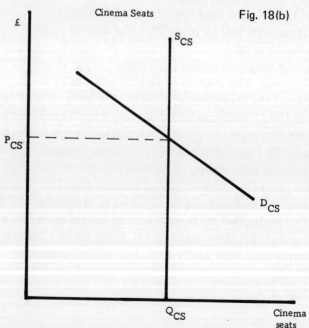

Cinema Seats   Fig. 18(b)

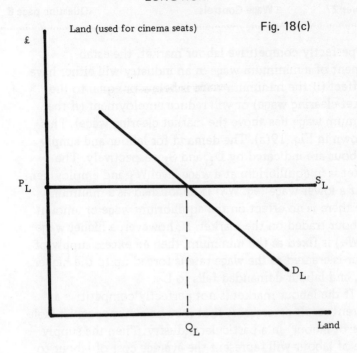

Land (used for cinema seats)   Fig. 18(c)

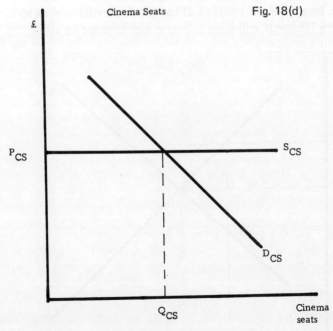

Cinema Seats   Fig. 18(d)

In a perfectly competitive labour market, the establishment of a minimum wage in an industry will either have no effect (if the minimum wage is below or equal to the market clearing wage) or will reduce employment (if the minimum wage lies above the market clearing wage). This is shown in Fig. 19(a). The demand for labour and supply of labour are indicated by D_L and S_L respectively. The market is in equilibrium at a wage level W_1 and employment L_1. If a lower wage (eg. W_2) is established as a minimum wage there is no effect on the equilibrium wage or amount of labour traded on the market. If, however, a higher wage (eg. W_3) is fixed as the minimum, then an excess supply of labour is created as the wage rate is forced up to the higher level, and labour demanded falls to L_2.

If the labour market is not perfectly competitive a different result emerges. A firm may be a monopsonist (sole buyer of labour) in a particular industry. Then the supply curve of labour will represent the average cost of labour to the firm (wage per employee). If the monopsonist wishes to hire more labour it will have to pay a higher wage to all

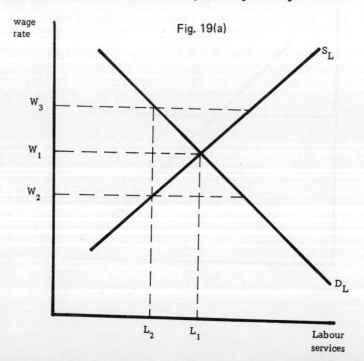

Fig. 19(a)

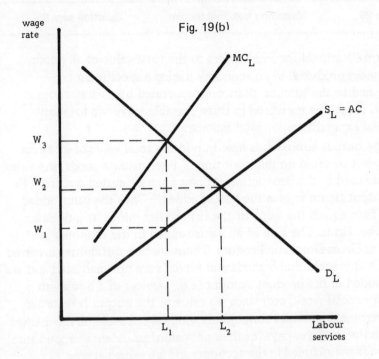

Fig. 19(b)

employees. The marginal cost of hiring additional labour is
then greater than the average cost. This is shown on
Fig. 19(b). If the firm equates marginal cost (MC_L) with its
demand (D_L) it will reduce both employment (L_1) and the
wage level (W_1) compared with the competitive equilibrium
(W_2 and L_2). Government establishment of a minimum wage
in this case can increase employment as well as the wage level
(provided the minimum wage chosen lies between W_1 and
W_3). This is the same result that would follow if a Trade
Union rather than the government established a minimum
wage[1]. So if the government establishes W_2 as the minimum
wage, employment is maximised at the competitive equilibrium (L_2).

In the long-run, the establishment of a high minimum
wage is likely to encourage the substitution of capital equipment for labour. This will lower the long-run demand for
labour and cause further reductions in employment.

[1] See the answer to Q. 25 for further elaboration.

The term "National Income" refers to the total value of all goods and services produced in an economy during a specific time period, and to the total of all income generated by such economic activity. It may be measured in three possible ways, via total output, total expenditure, or total income.

The output approach is based upon the total value of all firms' output, but to avoid double counting of intermediate goods, the value of inputs used in the production process must be netted out from the total output figure to give the "value added". Thus the value added by any firm equals the value of the firm's sales minus its purchases from other firms. The sum of all values added in the economy is known as Gross Domestic Product. There are two difficulties involved with this approach. Some goods and services are not marketed and are not included in the product account (e.g., services of a housewife, voluntary social work, etc) since no value of the output is recorded. The government provides some goods which are not sold on the market although the taxpayer pays for their provision (e.g. defence expenditure). Such goods are included in the accounts and are valued at cost.

Two further operations are necessary to convert Gross Domestic Product into National Income. Firstly net property income from abroad must be added. Basically this is income accruing to residents of the economy due to non-domestic activity minus income produced in the domestic economy accruing to non-residents. This calculation provides a figure for Gross National Income. During the course of production some current output must be used to replace worn-out capital equipment (depreciation). Subtracting this value of depreciation from Gross National Income leaves National Income.

A second way of obtaining this value is to consider the sum of all incomes earned by the owners of the factors of production. Adding together wages and salaries, profits, rent and interest gives a value for total income but stock appreciation (which by accounting convention is included as part of profits) must be netted out (since no production has occurred) before we obtain Gross Domestic Income. As with the output measure adding net property income from abroad and subtracting depreciation gives National Income.

The expenditure method involves the calculation of all expenditure made on the Domestic Product. Gross Domestic

Table 1

National Income Accounts

(i) OUTPUT	(ii) INCOME	(iii) EXPENDITURE
Output analysed by sector	Income from employment and self-employment + Profit and surpluses + Interest + Rent - Stock appreciation	Consumers' expenditure + Gross domestic fixed capital formation (investment) + Government expenditure + Value of physical increase in stocks + Exports less imports - Taxes on expenditure + Subsidies
Gross Domestic Product at factor cost + Net Property Income from abroad (NPI)	= Gross Domestic Income at factor cost + NPI	= Gross Domestic Expenditure at factor cost + NPI
Gross National Product - depreciation	= Gross National Income - depreciation	= Gross National Expenditure - depreciation
National Product	= National Income	= National Expenditure

Expenditure therefore equals the expenditure by households, domestic firms and the government plus exports minus imports. Two further modifications are necessary before we arrive at a figure consistant with the income and output measures considered above. Firstly we must add the value of the physical increase in stocks and work in progress. This represents unsold output which in the National Accounts is allocated as unintended investment expenditure by firms to ensure total expenditure equals total output. The second adjustment required is to net out the value of indirect taxes (less subsidies) from total expenditure to obtain a value for Gross Domestic Expenditure at factor cost. The existence of indirect taxes (or subsidies) cause market prices to be higher (or lower) than the costs of production or factor incomes. Finally, adding net property income from abroad and subtracting depreciation gives National Income.

Table 1 shows how these three sets of accounts are typically presented and the relationships between them.

Answer 29   Interpreting National Income   Question page 8

Gross Domestic Product at factor cost (GDP) is the amount of goods and services produced in an economy, and is usually taken to be the simplest available measure of social welfare. There are, however, several reasons why it is not a good measure and should not be used to judge welfare changes.

Firstly the Gross Domestic Product measures the total money value of final goods and services produced. Its value therefore has both a price and quantity element. Changes in either will cause the Gross Domestic Product to alter. If all prices in the economy doubled (including the price of labour), then welfare might remain unchanged, but the value of Gross Domestic Product would be doubled. To allow for the effect of such price changes on Gross Domestic Product we must adjust it by means of a price index, called the Gross Domestic Product Deflator. After this adjustment is made we have a value for Gross Domestic Product at constant prices.

Secondly, welfare depends not only on the size of Gross Domestic Product but also on the number of individuals in the society it is divided between. For a given value of Gross Domestic Product, welfare will be higher if there is a smaller population than if it were larger. Thus a better measure of welfare would be Gross Domestic Product divided by the total population, known as Gross Domestic Product per capita.

Related to this is the effect of income distribution on welfare. By using Gross Domestic Product as a measure of welfare, we are implicitly valuing money spent by a rich man on a luxury good as the same as an identical amount spent by a poor man on his necessities. This may be incorrect as the rich man's valuation of £1 will usually be much less than that of the poor man. Changing the distribution of income while holding Gross Domestic Product constant will alter social welfare but we are not able to say unequivocally whether it increases or decreases.

Thirdly, and perhaps most importantly there are a large number of omissions of goods and services from the recorded values of Gross Domestic Product. These can be subdivided into two groups; illegal activities, and non-marketed economic activities. Gross Domestic Product does not measure illegally produced output, even though some members of society may value it highly. Soft and hard drugs production and distribution, and prostitution are two obvious examples of illegal goods and services which are not recorded as Gross Domestic Product. Non-marketed economic activities, such as the work of a housewife, or home-grown garden produce increase welfare but are not recorded in Gross Domestic Product because they do not pass through a market. These two categories suggest that the officially recorded value of Gross Domestic Product is an underestimate of total economic activity.

Fourthly, there are a number of factors which contribute towards welfare that are not included in Gross Domestic Product. Leisure is highly valued, but a reduction in the working week will tend to reduce Gross Domestic Product whilst ignoring the impact of increased leisure time on welfare. Pollution of one kind or another is often an unwanted by-product of industrial production. If there are no restraints on smoke, fumes, dirt or noise then the gain in welfare following an increase in industrial production may be some extent be offset by a higher level of pollution.

To conclude, we may observe that Gross Domestic Product does not measure welfare properly, for it was never designed to do so. The National Income Accounts are statements about outputs of certain goods and services traded in markets in the economy during a particular period. It is thus a measure of "market activity" rather than welfare. Changes in the level of market activity alone should not be used to indicate welfare changes.

Answer 30 **Consumption** **Question page 8**

The most important influence on an individual's consumption expenditure is his level of income. This hypothesis was postulated by Lord Keynes in the General Theory (1936) as follows:
"The fundamental psychological law upon which we are entitled to depend with great confidence both a priori from our knowledge of human nature and from the detailed facts of experience, is that men are disposed as a rule and on the average, to increase their consumption as their income increases, but not by as much as the increase in their income."

The aggregage level of consumption is the sum of each individual's consumption, and this depends not just on the sum of individual incomes (aggregate income) but also on how this is distributed among households. For if different households have different propensities to consume (as is consistent with empirical observation), then different distributions of the same total income will give different levels of aggregage consumption.

Having determined that aggregage consumption depends upon income it is necessary to define the appropriate concept of income. National Income is not usually the best choice since it is disposable income that constrains household consumption. Disposable income is National Income minus direct taxes and other stoppages from pay. Thus changes in these taxes and stoppages will be expected to affect aggregate consumption also.

There are problems in using disposable income as the key influence on consumption. If households relate their consumption over time to some longer-term concept of income or wealth then short-term fluctuations in disposable income (caused, say, by temporary cuts in income tax) may not affect consumption as they are not expected to persist.

Apart from income, several other variables exert an influence on aggregate consumption. Variations in the availability and cost of credit can be expected to affect consumption especially as many items of consumer durables are purchased on credit. Restrictions on the availability of credit, such as increasing deposit requirements or increasing the cost of credit, in effect the rate of interest payable on credit sales (which is loosely-linked to the government determined minimum lending rate) both tend to reduce aggregate consumption and in particular consumer durables.

The volume of liquid assets (such as building society deposits, monetary savings etc.) may also have an impact on consumption expenditure. If during a credit squeeze households are unable to purchase consumer durables they may be forced to accumulate liquid assets. When credit conditions improve there may be a sudden increase in expenditure financed by a running down of these monetary savings.

Another factor influencing consumption expenditure is the expected level of inflation. If households expect prices to rise dramatically then they may bring forward purchases of consumer durables that they originally anticipated making only some time in the near future. Conversely, if prices are predicted to fall, households can be expected to postpone purchases as long as possible so as to enjoy lower prices.

Apart from economic variables affecting consumption there are a range of social and psychological considerations. Mass advertising the "benefits" of a materialistic society and maintaining social position by displaying high levels of consumption are two such non-economic influences on consumption. These influences are slow to change over time and do not affect short-term consumption plans. However, in the longer-run they may have a much larger impact.

Investment is the flow of expenditure on the production of new capital goods (houses, factories, machinery, etc.) or on net additions to stocks (raw materials, retail stocks, etc.). It is important to note that this is different from the layman's interpretation of investment when money is used to purchase a financial asset (building society deposit or securities).

Both the public and private sectors of the economy undertake investment projects but their motives may not be identical. Private sector investment is geared towards profitability and increased sales, whereas in the public sector more emphasis is placed on the social benefits of investments (better hospitals, schools,roads) although financial considerations are also important. In the private sector, business investment is the largest component and there are a number of theories about how this is determined.

For a single investment project, say a new machine, the entrepreneur will have made some calculation of the expected output from the machine and its likely selling price in order to estimate the revenue generated over time. Given the price of the machine and its expected running costs (maintenance, raw materials, labour) he is in a position to calculate the yield on the project. This is the rate of discount which equates expected revenues generated over the life of the machine to its costs. This rate of discount is known as the Marginal Efficiency of Capital (MEC). Only if this MEC is significantly greater than the cost of borrowing funds should the entrepreneur buy the machine.

At the aggregate level each project has an associated MEC. If all firms have access to borrowing funds at the going market rate of interest, r_o, then all projects which have a MEC above r_o would constitute the desired level of the capital stock. This is shown in Fig. 20 at K^*_o. Comparing this level with the existing capital stock, K_o we can find the desired change in the capital stock, $K^*_o - K_o$. It is usually assumed that the rate of investment expenditure is related to the desired change in the capital stock (although problems of capacity constraints or excess capacity may weaken this link). Thus, generally the greater the desired increase in the capital stock, the greater the level of investment. An increase in the expected revenue would shift the MEC schedule upwards say to MEC_2, raise the desired change in the capital stocks to $K^*_1 - K_o$

Fig. 20

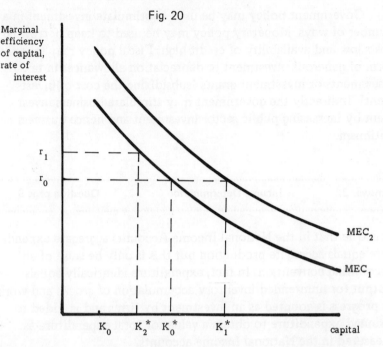

and so increase investment. This increase in expected revenue could be generated by increased business optimism concerning aggregate expenditure and profits. This would link aggregage investment expenditure to the level of income and profits in the economy. A rise in the rate of interest from r_0 to r_1 would reduce the desired change in the capital stock to $K^*_2 - K_0$. In this case the level of investment would be expected to fall. A rise in the cost of capital goods would lower the MEC and also cause investment to fall.

Investment expenditure may not only be linked to the level of income but to its rate of change, according to the accelerator theory. The line of reasoning is as follows: When income is rising the entrepreneur will invest to increase productive capacity; while income is constant at any level, entrepreneurs will only undertake replacement investment; while income is falling they may not even need to do this. Thus investment depends on changes in income rather than the level of income. However, there are several criticisms of this approach. Firstly, temporary fluctuations in demand should not be expected to lead firms to increase productive capacity which later may be left idle. Secondly, firms may choose to carry some spare productive capacity and allow fluctuations of demand to vary the usage of their existing capital equipment rather than invest.

Government policy may be used to stimulate investment in a number of ways. Monetary policy may be used to keep borrowing costs low and availability of credit high. Fiscal policy may take the form of generous investment or depreciation allowances in tax assessments or investment grants (subsidizing the cost of investment). Indirectly the government may stimulate business investment by increasing public sector investment and hence business optimism.

Answer 32   **Income Determination**   **Question page 9**

It is true that in the National Income Accounts aggregate expenditure equals aggregate production but this is only because of an accounting convention. In fact, expenditure identically equals output for unintended inventory accumulation of stocks and work in progress is counted as an investment by firms and is added to planned expenditure to obtain a value for total expenditure as measured in the National Income accounts.

In determining the equilibrium level of income we are not concerned with accounting identities but with planned behaviour. Only when aggregate planned expenditure is equal to aggregate output is the economy in equilibium.

In any period planned expenditure may differ from output. If say planned expenditure was less than output then firms would be left with unsold stocks. They would respond to this situation by reducing their level of output next period and thus aggregate income would fall. This fall in income induces a fall in expenditure but this is less than the fall in income so that the discrepancy between expenditure and output is reduced next period. This process continues until planned expenditure equals output in which case the economy returns to equilibrium.

Although not directly observable in the National Accounts, a disequilibrium situation can manifest itself through the figures for changes in stocks and work in progress. Since this component tends to be quite volatile in most economies, it seems to suggest that equilibrium is a rarity. Thus although actual expenditure always equals output, planned expenditure seldom does.

a)   An increase in the level of investment will raise the level of planned demand in the economy. If there are unemployed resources available which firms may hire to increase production, then income and employment will both rise as firms increase output to meet the higher level of aggregate demand. This initial rise in income will induce further consumption spending by households whose income have increased. The total effect on aggregate incomes is then larger than the initial rise in investment expenditure. The ratio of the change in income to the change in investment which brought it about is called the multiplier. The size of the multiplier is related to the size of the marginal propensity to consume (MPC) which is the proportion of any increase in income which households spend on consumer goods and services. The relationship is as follows:

$$\text{multiplier} = \frac{1}{1 - \text{MPC}}$$

If the MPC equals ¾ then the multiplier is 4. In this case an increase in investment of £100 would increase income by £400. Since we have the capacity to expand production we can assume prices are constant. We also assume that monetary conditions affecting expenditure are unchanged so there is no feedback say from changes in the rate of interest on investment expenditure. This situation is shown in Fig. 21. Initially the economy is in equilibrium below full employment at an income level Y_1 where the planned expenditure line E_1 cuts the equilibrium 45° line $E = Y$.

    An increase in investment raises the planned expenditure line to E_2 by the actual amount of the increase in investment. As firms increase output to meet the higher level of demand income will rise until a new equilibrium is found at Y_2, where E_2 cuts the equilibrium 45° line.

b)   The economy is already at full employment. An increase in investment will again raise the level of aggregate demand, but since there are no available resources to increase production the result will be an inflationary gap. On the diagram, let us now consider Y_1 to be the full employment level of output. When planned expenditure increases to E_2, the excess of planned expenditure over output is shown by AB which measures the size of the inflationary gap. This pressure of demand forces prices to rise.

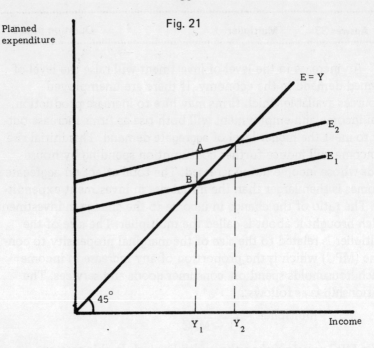

Fig. 21

They will keep rising until planned expenditures fall again to the full employment level of output. This price rise must be just sufficient to move the planned expenditure curve back to its former position E_1. At this level of expenditure the economy returns to equilibrium with the same level of real income Y_1 at the full employment level, but with a higher level of prices. This contrasts with the results derived in case a) when real output was increased and prices remained constant.

The government's budgetary position depends upon the difference between its receipts from taxations and its expenditure. If receipts exceed expenditure the budget is in surplus, if they are equal the budget is balanced and if receipts fall short of expenditure the budget is in deficit. Variations in the budgetary position may be employed to influence aggregate planned expenditure and so affect income and employment.

If the economy is in a recession with income below its full employment level, then the government should raise its expenditure and/or cut the level of taxation to cause a budget deficit and stimulate expenditure. Fig. 22 shows the planned expenditure line E_1 intersecting the equilibrium 45° line at Y_1 below the full employment level of Y_F. The deflationary gap AB indicates the amount by which planned expenditure falls short of output. By running a sufficiently large deficit to stimulate planned expenditures by the amount AB to E_2 the government can achieve full employment equilibrium. Note that a given increase in planned expenditure will require a larger budget deficit if taxes are cut than if expenditure is raised. This is because government expenditure raises planned expenditure directly, whereas tax cuts increase disposable income, part of which is spent and part of which is saved.

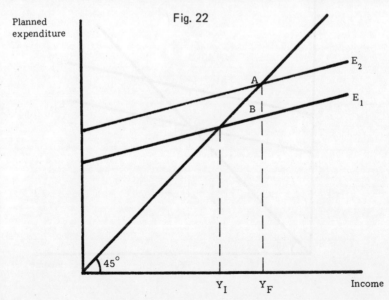

Fig. 22

If an inflationary gap exists with planned expenditure exceeding full employment output, the government can cut its expenditure and raise taxes to eliminate it. Fig. 23 shows planned expenditure at E_1, giving an inflationary gap CD. Using a budget surplus of appropriate size the government can reduce planned expenditure to E_2, restoring full employment equilibrium.

One advantage of fiscal policy is that there are a number of automatic stabilizers which tend to counteract fluctuations in economic activity. A progressive tax system and unemployment benefits are two examples of automatic stabilizers. When income falls tax revenue falls and unemployment benefits rise, generating a budget deficit to partially offset the recession.

The opposite effect occurs when income rises. The advantages of such stabilizers may be partially offset when discretionary fiscal policy is employed during a serious depression. In this case these stabilizers would make recovery from the depression more difficult. This is known as fiscal drag.

The simple predictions regarding the effect of fiscal policy may be confounded by a variety of reasons. An increase in government expenditure may crowd out some private expenditure that

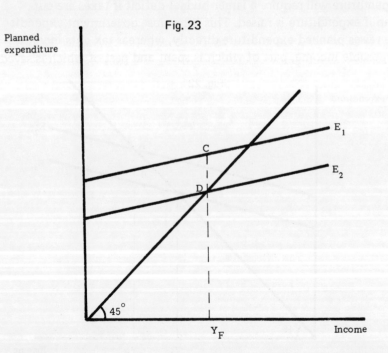

Fig. 23

might otherwise have occurred leaving planned expenditure at a lower level than anticipated.

An increase in government expenditure may be financed in three different ways: firstly by raising taxes, secondly by borrowing and thirdly by increasing the money supply. The method of finance may significantly affect the magnitude of the change in the planned expenditure.

The effects of fiscal policy may be difficult to predict in practice because small changes in government policy may lead entrepreneurs to revise their expectations about the future course of the economy, sometimes quite drastically.

Finally as with other policy instruments there are dynamic problems of timing. Any change in fiscal policy takes one to two years (or longer) to work through the economy, by which time the economic situation may have changed considerably. This has led some economists to abandon fiscal policy as a macroeconomic weapon. However this may be an extreme view, and most economists believe there is still a major role to be played by budgetary stabilization policy.

Money performs several essential functions in a modern developed market economy: a medium of exchange, a unit of account, and a store of value. Different types of assets carry out these functions more or less efficiently and this leads to difficulties in isolating one group of assets to bear the label 'money'.

The prime function of money is to act as a medium of exchange, i.e. to be generally acceptable in payment for goods and services. The desirable physical attributes of a transactions medium include durability, portability, and divisibility. Many items satisfy these criteria but are not used as money because they do not satisfy two economic requirements. Firstly, the circulating medium must be a scarce commodity in order to have a non-zero price (in terms of commodities). Secondly the opportunity cost of the asset used as money should be low (to minimise resources used in the production of money).

By far the majority of transactions in the U.K. involve the use of just two assets: legal tender and chequeable bank deposits. Legal tender (U.K. banknotes and coin) is a liability of the Central Bank (Bank of England) and almost universally acceptable as a means of payment in the U.K. Bank-notes are scarce (their supply is controlled by the Bank of England) and their opportunity cost is low (the cost of paper, ink and printing is small relative to their exchange value as £1 notes). Chequeable bank deposits (current accounts) are generally acceptable for most transactions and are the liabilities of the commercial banks. These too are scarce assets (the control of bank deposits is one aspect of monetary policy) and have a low opportunity cost (paper and/or computer tape). Other assets may be taken in exchange for specific transactions (eg. part-exchange) but are generally not acceptable. From its medium of exchange function it is now possible to provide a first operational definition of money (M_1) as: notes and coins in circulation plus sterling current account (chequeable) bank deposits held by the private sector.

The second function of money, as a unit of account, actually requires no physical commodity to circulate. Any common measure of the value of goods and assets can perform this function.

of the value of goods and assets can perform this function (eg. the U.K. guinea). This unit of account then allows economic agents to compare the relative prices of any two goods by comparing the value of one (in terms of the unit of account) with the other. Any significant change in the value of the unit of account relative to all other goods would necessitate a review of the valuations of each good in terms of the unit of account. As this may prove expensive to undertake (in terms of time and effort) it is desirable that the value of the unit of account remains relatively stable.

A definition of money based on this function requires only a unit of measurement (eg. £1) and not categories of assets. It is however convenient to have the same units for measuring value as are involved in the circulating medium. Thus nearly all commodities and assets have monetary values expressed in sterling.

The third function of money is as a store of value. Purchasing power may be held over from one period to another by holding assets of one kind or another. Money is a special kind of asset which has two characteristics: liquidity and (nominal) capital certainty. Liquidity is a property of an asset that is easily and quickly exchanged for all other commodities. Capital certainty implies a constant valuation of the asset in terms of the unit of account (but not necessarily in terms of purchasing power). There are many assets which possess these attributes to a greater or lesser extent. Legal tender and chequeable bank accounts are both perfectly liquid and capital certain. But deposit accounts with commercial banks, building society deposits, and some National Savings deposits are all capital certain and have a very high degree of liquidity. Therefore, an operational definition of money on this basis could include these assets, and any others possessing high liquidity and capital certainty. This definition would then be considerably wider than that obtained above from its function of medium of exchange. Indeed all assets can be ranked in descending order of both liquidity and capital certainty, so that it may be extremely difficult in practice to determine a boundary line between money and near money stores of value.

The problems of reconciling alternative functional definitions have resulted in two different official series of statistics for the money supply. M_1 is a narrow definition based on the circulating medium (defined above). M_3 is a broader definition related more generally to purchasing power which included M_1 plus all other bank deposits (sterling and non-sterling) held by U.K. residents in both the private and public sectors. The official statistics acknowledge that a functional definition of what is money is dependant on the particular function chosen, and hence it is impossible to agree on one definition of money which serves uniquely as both a circulating medium and store of value.

Answer 36　　　　　**Central Bank**　　　　　Question page 10

The supply of money is related to both the amount of legal tender (notes and coin) in circulation and the volume of bank deposits. The quantity of notes and coin is not a direct policy weapon - the Bank will generally meet any demand from the commercial banks. This means that controlling the money supply is a matter of regulating the volume of commercial bank deposits.

Since the 1971 change in the framework of monetary policy represented by Competition and Credit control, the commercial banks have been required to hold 12½% of their eligible liabilities in reserve assets. Their eligible liabilities are all sterling bank deposits except those with an original term to maturity of over two years. Reserve assets comprise balances at the Bank of England (excluding Special Deposits), Treasury Bills, Money at call, British government securities with less than one year to maturity, eligible local authority bills and eligible commercial bills (up to a maximum of 2% of the total). The central bank could change the minimum ratio in order to control the money supply but in practice relies on the commercial banks, as profit maximisers, to be reasonably near their minimum reserve ratio. Therefore by changing the reserve assets base of the banking system the Bank of England can cause a multiple expansion or contraction of commercial bank deposits and hence control the money supply.

usually pay with a cheque drawn on his current account made
payable to the Bank of England. This reduces the commercial bank's
balances at the Bank of England, which form part of their reserve
assets. Similarly, by buying government securities the Bank of
England may increase the commercial banks balances at the Bank of
England.

A second method of controlling the level of reserves is to
convert short-term government debt into longer-term debt. This is
known as funding. If the government reduces the Treasury bill issue
or buys short-dated government securities with less than a year to
maturity (both components of reserve assets) and increases sales of
medium to long-term debt (not reserve assets) then the commercial
banks' total reserve assets will fall if they cannot obtain replacement
reserves.

Special deposits constitute a third method of control over the
level of bank reserves. The Bank of England may ask the commercial
banks to deposit a certain proportion of their eligible liabilities at
the Bank in a special account. These deposits are not counted as
reserve assets. Hence the commercial banks must reduce their
holdings of other assets in order to meet the call for special deposits.

Aside from these measures the authorities have periodically
used direct methods of control over the activities of the commercial
banks to restrict the growth of the money supply, eg. setting
maximum rates of interest payable on bank deposits, specifying a
maximum growth rate for interest-bearing eligible liabilities (the
corset), or requesting the banks to cut their loans to specific sectors.
In addition the Bank may use changes in minimum lending rate as a
signal to indicate a desired change in the general interest rate
structure, and hence monetary conditions.

In theory the above controls over bank reserves could enable
the Bank of England to control the money supply quite accurately,
but in practice there are a number of limiting constraints. Firstly if
the commercial banks reserve asset ratio is some way above the
minimum level of 12½%, then substantial sales of gilts may be required to mop up this excess liquidity and curb monetary growth.
This may have unfavourable effects on the rate of interest. Also, if
the banks are holding excess liquidity because no-one wishes to take
up bank loans during a depression, then buying gilts to expand
reserve assets may have little effect on the money supply if these
extra deposits at the Bank of England cannot be turned into more
profitable assets.

Secondly the extent to which the commercial banks reserve assets can be squeezed depends on their ability to find adequate substitutes. If the financial system can easily generate their own reserves to combat a reduction in the Treasury Bill issue for example, then the restrictive activities of the Central Bank are futile and have no impact on the supply of money.

There are international considerations which limit the extent of the central bank's control over the money supply. Purchases or sales of sterling on foreign exchange markets undertaken by the Bank of England to support a specified exchange rate scheme may have domestic repercussions which will make control of the money supply difficult. Also interest-rate policy may be partly determined by the strength of sterling on foreign exchanges. During a crisis minimum lending rate may be raised substantially to attract capital inflows. This would exert a restrictive pressure on the money supply which may be undesirable from domestic considerations of economic policy.

Finally the effectiveness of the Bank of England to control the money supply is limited by the government's fiscal policy. If a large budget deficit is run, then the government will either raise the necessary funds by borrowing from the private sector (driving up interest rates) or borrowing from the Central Bank (increasing the money supply). The larger the budget deficit, the more likely this will then be accompanied by monetary expansion, and a consequent loss of control of the money supply.

In a fractional-reserve banking system, where commercial banks
are obliged to keep only a proportion of their deposit liabilities as
cash and selected reserve assets, the banks may acquire other assets
in exchange for some of the cash deposited with them. Assuming the
banks are profit-maximisers, they will not choose to hold excess
cash which offers a zero nominal return while other more profitable
assets are available, such as loans to individuals and companies, or
government securities. If there is sufficient demand for bank loans
at the going rate of interest then the banks have an incentive to
remain close to their minimum reserve ratio of 12½%. In this situation
they can only increase their loans by reducing their holdings of other
assets (eg. government securities)or by attracting a greater volume of
deposits. If the proportions of alternative assets held by banks
remains relatively constant then it is correct to state that new loans
can only be made when bank deposits rise. But this is not a justification for saying that the banks cannot create money, for in the
granting of loans, new deposits are created, giving rise to an increase
in the money supply.

   To see how this occurs, consider a simplified banking system.
Assume that; a) banks have two assets: cash - which earns no interest,
and loans - which earn a positive return; b) banks maintain a minimum
ratio of cash to deposits of 12½%; c) the supply of cash is determined
independently by a central bank; and d) the public's demand for cash
is constant. Suppose that one bank (Bank A) receives an additional
deposit of £10,000 generated by a central bank open market purchase of government securities. This increases its holdings of cash by
the same amount and therefore raises its reserves ratio above 12½%.
Bank A will increase profits by switching some cash into loans. To
observe the minimum reserve ratio the bank will have to hold only
12½% of the £10,000 increase in deposits, i.e. £1,250, as cash.
Therefore it can expand its loans by £8,750. Now, loans are given to
individuals and firms to finance expenditure. When the suppliers of
the goods and services purchased with the loan receive payment (in
the form of cheques drawn on the customer's account at Bank A)
they will deposit these at their own banks (since the public's demand
for cash is constant, the only way they can hold increases in money
balances is by depositing them in their bank accounts). Therefore
other banks now hold additional cash and deposits of £8,750 as a

direct consequence of Bank A's loan. As their reserve ratio is raised above the minimum they collectively need only keep 12½% of £8,750, i.e. £1093.75, as cash to maintain the 12½% reserve ratio. This leaves them free to expand loans by a further £7,656.25, creating further deposits and further loans. Eventually the process of deposit creation will cease when the total level of commercial bank deposits rises to eight times the initial increase in deposits made at Bank A i.e. to £80,000. Then the £10,000 initial deposit of cash is 12½% of the total generated deposits. Algebraically, if r is the reserve ratio, D the volume of bank deposits and C their reserves of cash then,

$$D = \frac{C}{r}$$

and a change in cash reserves ΔC will generate extra deposits ΔD as given by

$$\Delta D = \frac{\Delta C}{r}$$

so with ΔC = £10,000 and r = 12½% (= 0.125)

$$\Delta D = \frac{£10,000}{0.125}$$

$$= £80,000$$

This simplified picture does tend to overstate the ability of the commercial banks to create money. In practice the public's demand for cash will rise with an increase in income, so that not all of a loan is redeposited within the banking system. This cash drain reduces the ability of the banks to create further deposits.

Secondly the commercial banks do not always maintain their minimum legel reserve requirement. If they choose to hold excess reserves, or if they are unable to find individuals willing to take up their offers of loans then the initial increase in bank cash may have little effect on bank deposits and hence on the money supply. Consequently the ability of the commercial banks to create money may be somewhat impaired.

Finally, other financial institutions, such as the Building Societies, may compete for deposits with the commercial banks. If they succeed in attracting deposits away from the banks then again this will limit the ability of the commercial banks to create money. This effect may to some extent be offset if part of the loans made by other financial institutions generate new bank deposits.

In a modern developed economy money is required for two
main reasons. Firstly, a medium of exchange is needed to enable
economic units to trade efficiently. Since incomes and expenditures
are not synchronised, both individuals and firms must hold a stock of
money on which they may draw to make payments as required in
the period between income receipts. Such payments may involve
planned transactions (eg. weekly shopping, rent, etc.) or may be
unforseen (eg. accidental loss or breakages, bargain-offers etc). The
factors affecting the demand for such active balances are varied, but
basically relate to the value of transactions undertaken, or likely to
be undertaken per period, and the opportunity cost of money. The
value of transactions undertaken is dependent on the level of real
income and on the price level. The opportunity cost of money is the
nominal interest rate, which varies directly with the rate of inflation.

A rise in the rate of inflation will affect the demand for active
balances in two ways. Firstly, as the price level rises, more money
will be required to finance the same volume of transactions. Therefore the demand for nominal active money balances rises. Secondly,
the opportunity cost of holding money rises with inflation and
there is thus some incentive to economise on holdings of money
balances during the period between income receipts by temporarily
acquiring other assets whose returns rise with inflation. This would
suggest that the demand for real active balances falls with a higher
rate of inflation.

Money may also be held purely as a store of value. Since money
earns no interest the reason for holding such idle balances must be
related to its property of fixed nominal value. If other interest earning
assets are expected to fall in price, wealth-holders may prefer to hold
money rather than take a capital loss. This speculative motive is
inversely related to the current market rate of interest and expected
future asset prices. Given that current asset prices and effective
yields move in opposite directions for fixed interest bonds, then an
expected capital loss due to a fall in price will be associated with an
expected rise in the rate of interest. If wealth-holders have inelastic
bond-price expectations, then increases in the current price of bonds
caused by a reduction in the market rate of interest, will be

associated with increased fears of capital losses on bonds, and increase the demand for money.

An increase in the rate of inflation will increase the opportunity cost of holding such idle balances and therefore reduce the demand for real money balances held as an asset. However, as the value of non fixed-interest assets rises with inflation (nominal capital gains) so economic units may demand higher nominal idle money balances in expectation of possibly higher nominal capital losses.

In conclusion the effect of an increase in inflation is to raise the demand for nominal money balances (both active and idle components) but reduce the demand for real money balances.

Answer 39 **Monetary Policy** Question page 11

The demand for money is dependent, inter alia, on the level of real income and prices, and the rate of interest. If income and prices are held constant (at y_o and P_o) an inverse relationship may then be drawn between the demand for money and the rate of interest. This is shown as MD_o in Fig. 24. If the money supply is determined by the monetary authorities, then in the short-run its value is fixed and this may be represented as a vertical supply curve (MS_o) in the diagram. The equilibrium rate of interest is r_o, obtained by equating the demand for money with its supply.

Now if the monetary authorities reduce the money supply to MS_1 then for the current values of interest r_o income y_o and prices P_o there will be an excess demand for money, given by ($MS_o - MS_1$). Economic units want to hold more money than is presently available. This induces them to convert some of their holdings of highly liquid assets into money. The supply of such assets (e.g. bonds) is increased, driving their prices down, and hence the market rate of interest up. If we assume that income and prices remain constant then when interest-rate rises to r_1 the excess demand for money will be eliminated. The money market will be restored to equilibrium solely by variations in the rate of interest.

In this situation if the authorities control the money supply then the rate of interest will be determined by demand conditions. Conversely, if the authorities wished to keep the rate of interest constant they would have to give up control of the money supply. Therefore they are unable to control both.

This simplified view is unlikely to represent the real course of

Fig. 24

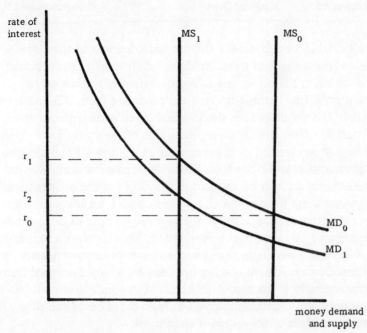

events for in practice income and the price level will almost certainly be affected by monetary conditions. Any reduction in the supply of money may directly cut consumption expenditure as well as forcing interest rates up. The rise in the rate of interest may reduce investment expenditure. Both factors would lower the level of demand in the economy, and hence prices and incomes. The effect on these two variables would be related to the existing level of unemployment. Reductions in prices or incomes lower the demand for money. If prices and incomes fall to P_1 and y_1, then the demand for money may shift to MD_1, following the original fall in the money supply. Thus in the diagram the effect of a reduction in the money supply is to raise the rate of interest, but only to r_2, which is less than r_1 obtained previously when prices and incomes were assumed to remain constant.

However this does not affect the previous conclusion that the monetary authorities can either control the money supply or the rate of interest. For again, if the money supply is held constant, then fluctuations in prices and incomes will shift the demand for money schedule, changing the equilibrium rate of interest. Also, if the authorities fix the rate of interest, then they must be prepared to supply as much money as is demanded, and hence lose control over the money supply.

The National Debt is basically the net indebtedness of the state to U.K. nationals and overseas holders. Additions to the National Debt arise when the government borrows money to finance its expenditure plans. If these borrowings are made from U.K. nationals then there is a simultaneous rise in holdings of assets (government securities) to offset the increased liabilities of the state. There is thus no change in net wealth in the economy as a whole. If foreigners buy U.K. government securities then the interest payments and capital repayments are a claim on the future resources of the economy, and in this sense some burden may be passed on to a future generation.

Servicing the existing debt is not generally a burden since interest payments may be raised through taxation. This involves a redistribution of income away from tax payers to holders of government securities. One very small burden imposed by a large National Debt held domestically is the resources involved in administering it (such as the labour and capital employed to raise extra taxes and pay interest to holders of government securities).

It is sometimes claimed that the National Debt is a burden because it allows the government to change the level of resources available to produce consumption and investment goods. If the government increases its spending on current goods and services by borrowing money which would otherwise have been used for investment purposes then the future capital stock will be reduced. This may reduce the rate of economic growth. But this is not a true burden for it is offset by the availability now of more consumption goods.

The National Debt may be a burden to the economy in a different sense, however, if it imposes a constraint on the operation of monetary policy. If the Bank of England is concerned with refinancing maturing debt, then it may wish to stabilise the prices of government securities and hence interest rates. This may seriously impair the ability of the Bank to control the supply of money, and weaken the ability of the government to implement its macroeconomic policies.

International trade takes place because of differences in opportunity cost or comparative advantage. Trading economies will benefit by producing and exporting those commodities in which they have comparative disadvantage. Therefore no country should lose by trading freely with another.

A country enjoys a comparative advantage when the opportunity cost of production (in terms of other goods) is lower than in other countries. Even if one country has a greater productivity than another in all commodities (i.e. enjoys an absolute advantage in all commodities) it will still benefit that country to specialise.

To simplify, consider two economies A and B, each capable of producing two goods X and Y. Let us assume that A is technically more efficient than B in both commodities (A has an absolute advantage over B). This means that A uses less resources to produce one unit of either X or Y than B. Superficially, it would seem that A should not trade with B, since B uses more resources in production. This is not correct, for the gains from trade are based on differences in opportunity costs, which are independent of any absolute advantages. Suppose the opportunity cost of producing one unit of Y in country A is sX, while in B it is tX, where s and t are constant. Without loss of generality, assume that s is greater than t. Then the opportunity costs of the two commodities in the two countries may be represented below:

Country	Opportunity cost of X	Opportunity cost of Y
A	$\frac{1}{s}y$	sX
B	$\frac{1}{t}y$	tX

$$\text{since } s > t, \frac{1}{s} < \frac{1}{t}$$

A has a comparative advantage in producing X and a comparative disadvantage in producing Y. In the situation before we introduce trade, both countries would have to produce both commodities. Now consider the effect of allowing them to specialise and trade. If B increases its production of Y by one unit (by reducing output of X by tX and A produces one unit less of Y (and uses the freed resources to produce an extra sX) then overall output of Y remains constant while output of X is raised by $sX - tX = (s - t)X$. Since s is greater than t, there is more X available, which can be

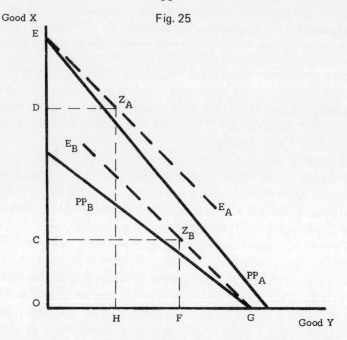

Fig. 25

distributed between the two countries. The rate of exchange will
determine the proportion of additional output going to each country
(i.e. who gains most from trade). Therefore no country has to lose by
trading with another. Both can gain.

This situation is depicted in Fig. 25. The two countries each
have a domestic production possibility curve, shown as PP_A and
PP_B respectively. The slope of these curves is constant, reflecting
the assumed constancy of opportunity costs. Country A specialises
in X and B in Y. With an international exchange rate between the
two opportunity costs then both countries gain by specialisation and
trade, as they may achieve combinations of both goods which lay
beyond their domestic production boundaries. In the diagram E_A
and E_B indicate the trading possibilities open to both countries
for a particular exchange rate. Thus country A could exchange an
amount ED of X for HO of Y to reach point Z_A. Consequently
country B has obtained an amount OC (equal to ED) of X for GF
(equal to HO) of Y to reach point Z_B.

In practice the assumption of a constant opportunity cost is not
valid. The law of diminishing returns would suggest that in the short
run opportunity costs rise as production of one commodity increases.
This implies that economies will only partly specialise in producing
goods until opportunity costs are equalised. In the longer run,
however, there may be economies of scale derived from specialization, which would increase the gains from trade.

The U.K. balance of payments accounts show the total value of
U.K. residents' financial transactions with the rest of the world.
Such transactions may involve goods and services, or physical and
financial assets.

The current account measures the difference between the value
of exports and imports of goods and services. It may be subdivided
into a balance of trade (net export of goods only) and the invisible
balances (net exports of services). The balance on the current
account is an important indicator of the solvency of a nation. If
there is a large deficit then imports exceed exports and the short-
fall must be financed by either acquiring additional liabilities or
reducing asset holdings. With a persistent deficit the government will
be forced to take remedial action to avoid bankruptcy. If the current
account is zero then the U.K. is financing imports via exports and
does not need to acquire additional liabilities. In this sense the balance of payments is in equilibrium when the current account is zero.
In 1974, the current balance was over £3,000 million in deficit,
which was a record. It is therefore this current account deficit to
which the first statement above refers.

In addition to transactions involving goods and services, there are
other monetary flows between U.K. residents and foreigners which
result from purchases and sales of U.K. and foreign assets. These
investments and other capital flows arise from various activities,
such as private investment overseas and overseas investment in the
U.K. private sector. Foreign acquisition of U.K. assets involves a
flow of money coming into the economy, and is represented by a
positive value in the accounts. On the other hand when U.K.
residents acquire foreign assets, this causes an outflow of money,
and consequently this is associated with a negative figure in the
accounts.

The current balance and the net investment and capital flow,
together with a small balancing item (reflecting non-recorded
transactions) give a figure for the total flow of currency into the
economy. If this figure is negative it indicates that the supply of
sterling (to finance imports of goods, services and acquisition of
foreign assets) exceeds the demand for sterling (to finance exports).
Under normal market conditions an excess-supply (or excess demand)
would lead to a price fall (price rise). Hence the value of sterling
would drop (rise) to eliminate the imbalance. But this need not

happen provided the government is willing to purchase the excess-supply of (meet the excess demand for) sterling at the current rate of exchange.

With government intervention in the foreign exchange market to stabilise the rate of exchange, the total currency flow is unlikely to be zero. The government must then finance this inflow or outflow. There are two basic methods. Firstly they may rely on drawings on (or additions to) the reserves of gold and foreign currency. Secondly they may make changes in the level of official borrowings from overseas monetary authorities.

When all financial transactions are totalled - from all sections of the accounts - the balance of payments must always be zero. Any excess spending on imports over receipts from exports give rise to a total currency outflow which is balanced by either reducing U.K. reserves or borrowing. In this accounting sense the second statement is correct by definition, but it is not a useful statement as it does not mean that the economy is in equilibrium. The concept of an equilibrium balance of payments must then always refer to a subset of the accounts, such as the current account.

Answer 43   **Exchange Rates**   Question page 12

Under a system of flexible exchange rates the equilibrium rate is determined in the market by demand and supply. The demand for sterling is a derived demand arising from U.K. exports of goods and services and foreign acquisition of domestic assets. The supply of sterling is derived from U.K. imports of goods and services and U.K. residents' acquisition of foreign assets. Both supply and demand depend on the foreign exchange rate. Under the assumption that the price elasticity of the demand for imports in the U.K. exceeds unity (import demand is elastic) the supply curve for sterling will slope upwards. The demand curve will normally slope downwards (unless demand for U.K. exports is completely inelastic when it is vertical). The equilibrium rate of exchange (e_1) is determined by the intersection of supply (S_1) and demand (D_1) in Fig. 26.

Fluctuations in the exchange rate will arise if demand and supply are not equal. Excess demand will cause the rate to rise and excess supply will cause it to fall. There are many factors which could cause shifts in these curves. An increase in world trade would increase exports and hence stimulate the demand for sterling, causing it to

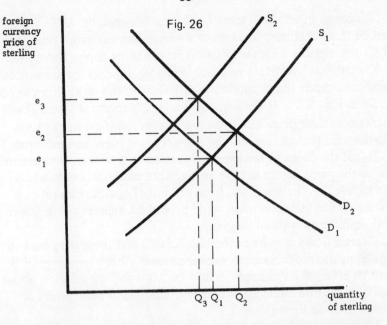

Fig. 26

shift to say D_2 on the diagram, and raising the equilibrium exchange rate to e_2. A relative increase in U.K. firms' productivity or an increase in the quality of British goods would tend to have a similar effect on exports. In addition they may encourage import-substitution and so shift the supply curve inwards to S_2. This would raise the equilibrium rate further still, say to e_3.

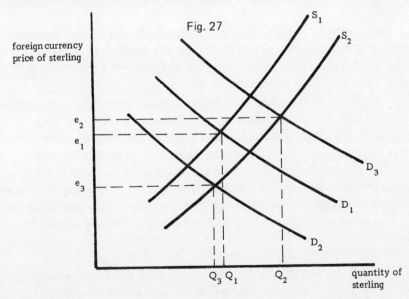

Fig. 27

A change in relative rates of inflation between the U.K. and the rest of the world may increase or decrease the exchange rate. If the U.K. experiences a higher inflation rate than its competitors then as U.K. residents substitute relatively cheaper imports for domestically produced goods the supply curve will shift to the right, from say S_1 to S_2 in Fig. 27. If the demand for U.K. exports is elastic, the increase in their price due to higher British inflation will reduce the demand for sterling and shift the original curve inwards from D_1 to D_2. If the demand for exports is inelastic, however, the demand for sterling will rise to say D_3 as the value of exports rises with the higher U.K. prices. Thus from an initial equilibrium rate e_1, differences in inflation rates could produce a higher (e_2) or lower (e_3) equilibrium rate of exchange.

Capital flows may be extremely volatile and these may lead to highly erratic movements in exchange rates. Short-term capital flow may be affected by changes in interest rates and speculation about capital gains due either to anticipated changes in asset prices or exchange rates themselves.

Variations in the exchange rate due solely to these short-term capital flows will affect the relative price of exports and imports. This may cause domestic instability. If the exchange rate falls then the demand for exports will rise and if the economy is operating at or close to the full employment level this could generate inflation. If the exchange rate rises then the demand for U.K. exports will fall and if factors of production are immobile then unemployment will result.

The government may choose to intervene in the foreign exchange market to stabilise the rate of exchange and avoid the problems associated with erratic short-term capital flows and factor immobilities. They also have another motive for this policy. If exchange rates are freely determined then importing and exporting firms may be uncertain about the future value of foreign currency earnings (exports) or foreign currency costs (imports) and may decline large orders or long-term contracts. Therefore governments may stabilise rates to help foster world trade, by reducing such uncertainty. In practice the existence of a forward market in sterling eliminates the risk of exchange loss, although this 'insurance' may prove costly.

The arguments against trying to stabilise the rate are related to three main factors. Firstly there are short-run difficulties of operating a stabilisation fund. To buy excess currency during a period of deficit may require substantial reserves of gold and foreign exchange. In the long run, it may be impossible to maintain an unrealistic par

value. Secondly, it may prove difficult to arrange a smooth altera-
tion in par values should such a fundamental disequilibrium situation develop. Thirdly, speculators may cause dramatic shifts in the
demand for and supply of currency. This may place intense short-
term pressure on the country's reserves, with a consequent need for
substantial international collaboration to withstand the pressure.

Answer 44   **External Imbalance**   Question page 12

Both depreciation and devaluation may improve a country's
balance of payments. However, the effects on the domestic economy
are not identical and therefore they cannot be considered as
equivalent policies. A deficit on the balance of payments implies
that there is an excess supply of sterling on the foreign exchange
markets. Exports of goods and services and acquisition of U.K.
assets by non-residents (or sale of foreign assets by U.K. residents)
give rise to a demand for sterling. In the same way imports of goods
and services and acquisition of foreign assets by U.K. residents (or
sales of U.K. assets by non-residents) generate a supply of sterling.
The existence of a balance of payments deficit therefore means that
more pounds are being supplied to the foreign exchange market than
are being demanded.

Depreciation involves a downwards movement of the exchange
rate (the foreign currency price of sterling). This makes exports
cheaper in terms of foreign currency, and imports dearer in terms
of sterling. If the demand for U.K. exports is responsive to these
price changes (i.e. demand is elastic) then an increased value of
exports will lead to a greater demand for sterling. Similarly if the
U.K. demand for imports is elastic then a rise in their price will
reduce the revenue of importing firms, and hence the supply of
sterling will fall. If capital flows remain relatively constant, then
depreciation will reduce the excess-supply of sterling and hence
improve the balance of payments.

The effect of depreciation on the domestic economy is to raise
the level of aggregate demand. This occurs because of the direct
stimulus to exports and also because the rising price of imports will
increase demand for domestically produced substitutes. If the
economy is at or near full employment this would impart an upward
pressure on prices. However, if there were unemployed resources

which could be quickly channelled into the exporting industries, the increase in aggregate demand would reduce the level of unemployment. Thus depreciation would not only improve the balance of payments, but would also improve employment levels.

Deflation involves the use of restrictive monetary and fiscal policies to reduce the level of aggregate demand. This improves the balance of payments in two ways. Firstly the lower level of economic activity results in fewer imports of goods and services. The higher the income elasticity of the demand for imports the greater the reduction in the level of imports resulting from a given reduction in aggregate income. Secondly, if restrictive monetary policy is employed the domestic rate of interest will rise. This may attract an inflow of capital from abroad as foreign wealth-holders buy British assets to obtain higher returns. Additionally the rise in domestic interest rates will reduce planned levels of investment and induce a further fall in aggregate demand and hence imports. If restrictive fiscal policy is used the domestic rate of interest may fall. This would tend to impair the effect on the balance of payments on two counts. The lower rate of interest may cause a capital outflow as foreign wealth-holders sell U.K. assets because of the low returns. Also the lower rate of interest may stimulate domestic investment. This could off-set (or even eliminate)the effects of the original restrictive fiscal policy. If the economy is at or close to the full employment level of activity then a policy of deflation may improve the balance of payments and not generate too high a level of unemployment. However, if the economy is already experiencing a recession then further deflation to improve the balance of payments will only add to the level of unemployment.

If the government maintains a fixed exchange rate during a deficit it must buy the excess sterling coming on to the foreign exchange market. This reduces the domestic money supply (unless the government sterilises this effect by open market purchases of government securities). The reduction in the money supply is itself deflationary so that no further restrictive fiscal action may need to be taken to depress the economy.

Depreciation and deflation rely on different causal mechanisms to restore balance of payments equilibrium. Depreciation works through changes in relative prices and is associated with increased aggregate demand whereas deflation works through a reduction in income and is consequently associated with a reduced level of economic activity. Therefore although both measures may improve external balance, they cannot be said to be equivalent.

The International Monetary Fund (I. M. F.) was established at
the Bretton Woods Conference in 1944, when the basis of the
international payments system was agreed. It began in operation in
1947, although it took several years to have a major impact. The
basic aim of the I.M.F. was to foster World Trade. It was to encourage
this in several ways.

Firstly, member countries were to establish par values for their
currencies in terms of gold, the dollar, or sterling, and maintain them
within 1% above or below this rate. Under fixed exchange rates
importing and exporting firms are more certain about the future
value of foreign currency earnings arising from exports and foreign
currency costs due to imports. This may encourage them to expand
business.[1]

If member countries maintain fixed external parities then they
must use alternative domestic methods to eliminate a balance of
payments deficit, such as deflationary monetary and fiscal policies.
In cases of a fundamental disequilibrium, however, member countries
were allowed to change the par value and the I.M.F. could give
financial assistance to allow this to be implemented in an orderly
fashion.

This rigid system of exchange rates was a major stumbling block
of the I.M.F. from 1967 (when Britain devalued) onwards. As
countries maintained different growth rates, and sustained different
rates of inflation, it became impossible to rely on domestic policies
to eliminate deficits without causing massive unemployment. In
addition, surplus countries were loath to revalue their currencies
for fear of inflation. The growth of a highly mobile sources of
short-term capital put intense speculative pressure on deficit
countries to devalue and made it difficult, if not impossible, for
them to maintain a fixed unrealistic exchange rate.

The second way in which the I.M.F. hoped to encourage trade
was by providing additional international liquidity. Each member
country was allocated a quota in accordance with its economic
importance and level of trade. This quota was paid to the I.M.F.
in gold (25%) and domestic currency (75%). They could then

[1] See the answer to Question 43 for further discussion of this
point.

borrow up to 125% of this quota from the fund in various tranches. The first 25% (the gold tranch) could be used automatically, but further credit tranches had increasingly strict conditions attached. Loans were to be prepaid within 3 to 5 years.

The rapid rise in the level of world trade in the last twenty years has required a vast increase in the quantity of international reserves. The I.M.F. increased quota subscriptions several times between 1959 and 1975 but this has not been sufficient. Other sources of international reserves have been developed both inside and outside the I.M.F. to compensate, e.g. the General Agreement to Borrow, Swap arrangements between central banks, and Special Drawing Rights. The dominant reserve asset is still, however, foreign exchange especially the dollar - and as new reserves of dollars may only be acquired if the United States runs a deficit, this was bound to lead to instability.

In the early 1970's the fixed exchange rate system collapsed and most major currencies were floating by 1973, either by themselves (independently) or aligned with others (e.g. the snake in the tunnel). The main cause of the collapse was the serious weakness of the dollar due to a fundamental balance of payments deficit. This encouraged speculation against the dollar. In December 1971, Finance Ministers from several countries tried to patch up the fixed exchange rate system by devaluing the dollar in terms of gold and revaluing certain other currencies. It was also decided to allow a wider variation (2¼%) of currency values about the dollar parity. This Smithsonian agreement was short-lived. The I.M.F. was powerless to prevent high speculative pressure against, first, sterling, which was eventually floated in June 1972, and then the dollar, which was further devalued in 1973.

Since then it seems the I.M.F. has learned the lesson that it is not possible to maintain fixed exchange rates by lending indefinitely to deficit countries. New loans, e.g. the one to U.K. in 1976, attract stringent conditions for getting the domestic economy into balance and hence reducing balance of payments deficits. The I.M.F. is still a very important source of international liquidity but cannot stabilise foreign exchange markets in the face of intense speculative pressure. It seems the I.M.F. must continue to accept a reduced role in the present situation until a new system of monetary cooperation is developed which can deal with the movement of large speculative balances.

A high level of unemployment indicates that the supply of
labour exceeds the demand for labour at a particular wage rate.
It is correct, therefore, to say that an increase in demand for the
particular type of labour in excess-supply would eliminate the
problem. In practice, the distribution of unemployment both
between regions and between industries is not even. Hence, an
overall increase in demand engineered by expansionary monetary
and fiscal policy may cause excess demand and inflationary pressures in some markets while still leaving substantial pockets of
unemployment in others. The unemployment problem is thus not
just one problem but several, because of the many different types
of unemployment and their separate causes.

Demand deficient cyclical unemployment arises because of a
general lack of purchasing power in the economy. During a recession
firms are pessimistic about future sales and hence cut production
and lay-off labour, thus reducing income. Consequently, expenditure falls even further. This type of unemployment may persist for
some time if prices and wages cannot adjust to restore overall
equilibrium. In such a case the government can adopt expansionary
policies to alleviate the short-fall of demand. Problems may still
arise if the expansion is undertaken too fast, for bottle-necks may
develop in key industries.

Structural unemployment is caused by a long-run shift in demand
away from a particular good. Over time, the market shrinks, the
industry contracts, and labour is made redundant. If similar firms
are situated together this creates a regional unemployment problem
as the industry goes into decline. It is not sensible to expand aggregate demand to cure such structural unemployment. Instead, policies
should be geared towards increasing the geographical and occupational mobility of the labour force. These may include: setting up skill-
centres to provide training for employment elsewhere in growth
industries; or offering financial contribution towards relocation
expenses; or just passing on information about jobs available.

A third form of unemployment is due to technical progress,
where new processes or capital innovations require different types
of skills from the labour force. A higher rate of economic growth
may be associated with the need for a more occupationally mobile
workforce. If workers are unable to acquire skills quickly to operate
the new equipment then technological unemployment may result.

It is also claimed that automation has reduced the demand for unskilled labour - their place being taken by complex machines operated by highly skilled labour. Policy designed to cure this type of unemployment is similar to that for structural unemployment.

Frictional unemployment is caused by short-run shifts in demand and supply. These result in relative changes in the demand for labour. If labour is unable to adjust quickly enough to these changes some unemployment will be generated. Government policies to improve the flow of information about job opportunities and retraining programmes may again improve the situation. If the immobility of labour continues into the long-run with no improvement in demand conditions this frictional unemployment will become the more difficult structural type.

The final type of unemployment is caused by seasonal fluctuations in the pattern of consumer demand, and hence factor demand. Labour becomes regularly unemployed during certain periods of the year although during others there may be excess-demand. A possible government policy might be to encourage the growth of another seasonal commodity whose peak period of demand matches the current peak period of unemployment. Such fortuitous circumstances are rare and government policies have not been concerned with this issue directly.

It is clear, then, that an expansion of aggregate demand is only a cure for one type of unemployment - that caused by a deficiency of purchasing power. Other types of unemployment cannot be tackled by this method and require particular policies designed to reduce labour immobility, both geographical and occupational. Therefore the above statement is correct.

Answer 47   **Inflation**   Question page 13

Inflation may be defined as a continuous rise in the average price level. This is caused by an excess of aggregate demand over aggregate supply in the economy, and is always associated with either an expansion of the money supply or an increase in the velocity of circulation. Being essentially a monetary phenomenon, inflation can be controlled by keeping the money supply under a tight rein, for there are limits to which its velocity can vary. However, this

solution may be associated with high unemployment levels.[1]
Inflation may also be controlled by Prices and Incomes Policies.
Here the primary effect may be to shift from an open inflation
(where prices rise in response to excess-demand), into a repressed
inflation (where the excess-demand persists but prices are not allowed
to rise). Such policies also have adverse effects on economic efficiency. Since they introduce rigidities into the price system, they fail
to allow the market to allocate resources and goods properly.

Let us consider an initial situation of constant prices with no
inflationary expectations. This situation is represented in Fig. 28
where aggregate demand (D_0) and aggregate supply (S_0) together
determine the price level (P_0) and output (Y_0). Either an increase
in aggregate demand to D_1, or a reduction in aggregate supply to
S_1, will generate excess - demand and a price rise to P_1 or P_2
respectively.

Fig. 28

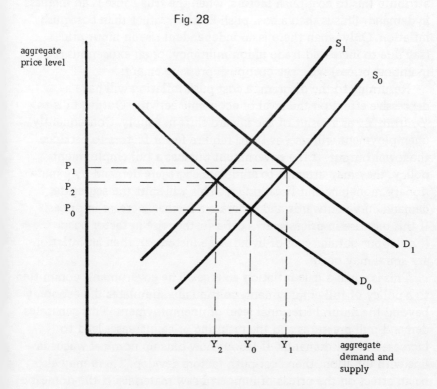

[1]·See the answer to question 48 for an explanation of the relationship between unemployment and inflation.

The Demand-pull theory argues that shifting demand conditions cause the price level to be pulled up. The cost-push argument is that rising costs shift the supply curve inwards and that this pushes the price level up. If no other changes take place then the once and for all price rise will eliminate the excess-demand. Consequently neither the demand-pull theory or the cost-push theory are sufficient by themselves to generate inflation, which as defined above is a continuous rise in prices.

In addition, much of a so-called cost-push increase in prices may, in practice, be due to demand-pull factors. Consider the effect of an increased demand for goods and services. Firms will need to hire more factors of production to raise output. If the economy is at, or close to, the full employment level, this increased factor demand will raise input prices. The same may also be true for raw materials. Therefore, firms will observe an increase in their costs, and may attribute this to cost-push factors, when the true cause is an increase in demand. This is then a cost-push illusion, rather than cost-push inflation. Only when there is an independent rise in input prices (say due to increased trade union militancy, or an exogenous rise in import prices) will true cost-push pressure emerge.

Returning to the diagram, a cost-push inflation will have a depressive effect on the level of economic activity. Output falls to Y_2 from Y_o as a result of the inward shift in supply. Consequently unemployment will rise, as firms require fewer factors to produce the lower output. If the government pursues a full employment policy, they may attempt to stimulate aggregate demand by expansionary monetary and fiscal policy. This will shift the aggregate demand curve outwards and generate a further increase in prices. If this increase in prices sparks off a further rise in factor costs (e.g. labour obtains cost-of-living wage increases), then an inflationary spiral may occur.

This is when a true inflation emerges. The government, committed to a policy of full-employment, continually stimulates the economy beyond the natural frictional level of unemployment. This generates demand-pull pressures and the resulting price increases lead to increased factor demands. If labour now bids up nominal wages in line with inflation, then cost-push factors develop. There may also be an effect on the prices of imported raw materials. If the domestic inflation rate exceeds that of U.K. competitors then the balance of payments will tend to go into a deficit on current account as imports become relatively cheaper and exports relatively dearer than foreign goods (although it is possible that no deficit will occur[2]). This deficit situation may be eliminated by a depreciation of sterling. This will raise import prices and stimulate further cost-inflation. The falling pound will also offset any reduction in the demand for exports caused by the domestic inflation. Thus demand and cost factors inter-react to generate an inflationary spiral, which is fuelled by the increase in the money supply associated with government expansionary policy.

Government attempts to eliminate inflation may break into the spiral at three points. Firstly they may control the nominal money supply. This will mean that the additional demand for money balances brought about by inflation creates an excess-demand for money. Generally, such a situation will cause the market rate of interest to rise, which will reduce investment expenditure (assuming it is responsive to interest rate changes). The reduction in aggregate demand will then eliminate the inflationary pressure by a contraction of demand.

Secondly, the government may attempt to control factor incomes, especially wages and salaries - a major component of costs in many industries. The objective here is to eliminate directly any domestic cost-push pressures. As prices rise, the excess-demand is eliminated by a reduction in real wages. This may involve a redistribution of income for firm's profits will generally rise as their costs fall.

Thirdly, the government may control the prices of domestically produced goods and services directly. This has little effect on demand apart from some redistribution of income from owners of firms to workers, if nominal wages rise. Supply is likely to be reduced as firms switch to non-controlled export markets. Price controls, then, will not eliminate the excess-demand condition, and may exacerbate the problem. As prices are not allowed to rise, the open inflation is replaced by a repressed inflation. In this situation shortages of goods and services are likely to develop throughout the economy. Quotas, or some other system of allocating goods to customers, must then be employed.

When these latter two policies are adopted simultaneously the excess-demand cannot be eliminated. Repressed inflation will emerge and since relative prices are fixed, the market system will be

---

[2] See the answer to question 43 for the explanation of the effect of domestic inflation on the rate of exchange.

prevented from performing its economic functions of allocation and distribution efficiently.

In conclusion the distinction between demand-pull and cost-push inflation is not generally useful, as most cost-push inflation amounts to a cost-push illusion due to demand-pull factors. Stabilising the rate of monetary growth is the only long-run solution to the problem of inflation, although this may involve a loss of employment temporarily. Prices and Incomes policies have little effect on inflation rates. Their other economic effects are detrimental to the efficient use of resources. Therefore they are not equivalent to monetary contraction as solutions to the problem of inflation.

Answer 48   **Phillips Curve**   Question page 13

The relationship between unemployment and inflation has been the subject of much debate among economists. Some agreement has emerged from the discussion to indicate a fairly stable short-run relationship based on the findings of Professor A.W. Phillips, but long-run conclusions differ according to alternative schools of thought. In 1958 Phillips published an empirical paper which testeu the hypothesis that wages rates rose faster when unemployment was low than when it was high. He discovered a very close correlation between wage inflation and unemployment in the U.K. between 1861 and 1957. Subsequently, these results were used to demonstrate the existence of a trade-off between price inflation and unemployment, since wage inflation and price inflation are highly correlated. The "Phillips curve" relationship, as it became known, is shown in Fig. 29. It seems to suggest that with productivity rising at around 2%, an unemployment rate of 2½% was required for price stability. Full employment was not consistent with price stability and some compromise had to be accepted. For example if it is desired to achieve an unemployment rate of only 1½%, then the cost of achieving this is an inflation rate of 3%. This tradeoff position is indicated as point A in Fig. 29.

The economic explanation for the existence of the Phillips curve depends on several assumptions. Firstly, if prices are fairly sticky downwards in all markets then an overall excess-supply of goods and services is likely to be associated with a fall in output and employment, rather than a reduction in prices. Secondly, if all markets exhibit varying levels of excess-demand, equilibrium, and excess-supply, then we may expect unemployment and inflation to co-exist. A rise in the overall level of demand throughout the economy would therefore reduce the number of markets experiencing excess-supply and hence reduce unemployment, but would increase the number of markets experiencing excess-demand and so generate a higher level of inflation. This analysis presumes that changes in nominal prices are seen as real price changes, i.e. in the labour markets, an increase in nominal wages is seen by the labour force as an increase in their real wages.

Fig. 29

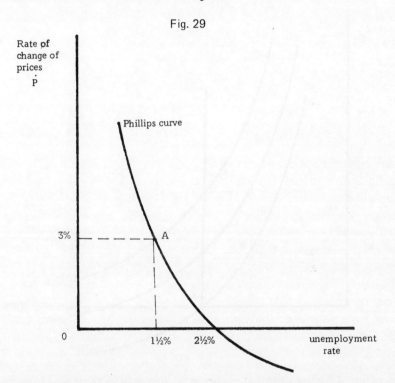

During the 1970s the observed values of inflation and unemployment rates failed to correspond with points on the Phillips curve. Unemployment rates which were associated with price stability ten years earlier were now being associated with double-figure inflation. Either the Phillips curve had been discredited or there was some important factor which had been responsible for causing a shift in the curve and had not been taken into account in the Phillips analysis. In the United States, Profs. M. Friedman and E. Phelps suggested why indeed this may have been the case. Their argument indicated that there was no long-run trade-off between inflation and unemployment.

Consider Fig. 30. The $SRPC_1$ curve represents the Phillips curve. Let us assume the economy is initially at point A, with unemployment at u_0 and zero price inflation. Suppose now the government aim to achieve the tradeoff represented by point B on the diagram, with unemployment at u_1 and price inflation at $\dot{P}_0$, by stimulating aggregate demand. In order to increase production (to meet the higher level of demand) firms will need to hire additional factors and will have to bid up nominal wages to achieve this. Workers see

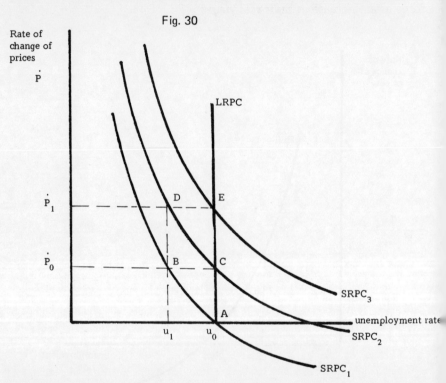

Fig. 30

the offer of higher nominal wages as an increase in their real income, for they are not yet aware of the existence of inflation. They will therefore increase the supply of labour, so that the level of unemployment initially falls from u_0 to u_1. However, in time workers observe that their higher nominal wages are accompanied by higher inflation ($\dot{P}_0$) so that their real wages are unaffected. Given that the supply of labour depends on the real wage and not the nominal wage then the labour supply will return to its original level, and unemployment will rise back to u_0. This is represented by point C, immediately above point A. In negotiating future pay settlements workers will add on the expected rate of increase of prices to their real pay demands. If the expected rate of inflation is determined by the present rate of inflation then, in effect, the short-run Phillips curve has shifted vertically upwards from $SRPC_1$ to $SRPC_2$.

Now if the government continue to aim for the level of unemployment indicated by u_1, they will need to stimulate aggregate demand still further. This will cause a similiar movement along $SRCP_2$ to point D. Eventually workers will come to accept $\dot{P}_1$ inflation as 'normal' and will add this to their pay demands. This will shift the SRPC upwards yet again, to $SRPC_3$. The short-run tradeoff between inflation and unemployment disappears in the long-run, according to this analysis. Any attempt to operate the economy below the natural rate of unemployment (defined as that rate consistent with no change in the rate of inflation) will only generate accelerating inflation. In the long-run the Phillips curve is vertical, and there is no tradeoff. This is represented by LRPC in Fig. 30.

This view has been challenged by some economists who argue that not all workers raise their wage demands fully in line with inflation. This argument would suggest that the long-run Phillips curve is not vertical, but certainly much more steeply sloped than the short-run curves.

There may be a further complication to the Phillips curve. The natural rate of unemployment may itself change over time. Given the structural changes that take place in the economy, the reduced opportunity - cost of unemployment, and the reduced efficiency of the price system with high levels of inflation, it may be impossible to specify the natural rate of unemployment. Consequently, even a short-run trade-off with inflation may be unstable.

Finally, if an inflationary situation persists for some time, then labour may revise their expectations of future inflation (and hence pay demands) more quickly. This would again reduce the stability of the short-run trade-off between inflation and unemployment.

In 1936 Lord Keynes published his 'General Theory,' which advocated the use of expansionary fiscal policy to eliminate the problem of demand-deficient unemployment. Such policy would involve an increased level of government expenditure and/or a reduction in taxation. The idea behind this was that the government should spend more than its tax revenue and cause a budget deficit to arise (or increase). This initial stimulus to expenditure would, via the expenditure multiplier, cause a greater increase in the level of aggregate expenditure. Firms would hire more labour to increase production and so unemployment would be reduced. Keynes further suggested that if the government did not intervene to increase aggregate demand, the recession would persist. This conclusion was based on the existence of wage and price rigidities in the real world. If firms were not willing to reduce their prices when demand for their product fell, and if labour was unwilling to take a cut in nominal wages when unemployment rose, then there seemed to be no way in which an economy could climb out of a recession.

Keynesian policies, essentially fiscal policy, have been used since the second world-war to meet the objective of full employment. Indeed, until the early 1970's this proved very effective. However, critics have argued that the objective of full employment is not compatible with either price stability or balance of payments equilibrium. They state that full employment is impossible to attain using only an expansion of aggregate demand, for there are many other types of unemployment which cannot be reduced by such a policy[1]. Thus government attempts to stimulate the economy to operate below the natural rate of unemployment (where demand deficient unemployment is zero) will put upward pressure on prices. In addition, if aggregate supply is relatively inelastic in the short-run, then the increased level of aggregate demand will tend to increase imports and reduce the supply of exports.

Keynesian policies may be perfectly compatible with price stability, however, if the aim of full employment is relaxed. Moreover if the government uses suitable alternative policies to deal success-fully with other types of unemployment (e.g. retraining schemes, relocation expenses, job-information services) this objective could

[1] See the answer to question 46 for a fuller discussion of this point.

still be met. The first statement is therefore not correct in theory, although in practice, the way in which fiscal policy has been used in the U.K. has contributed towards the current lack of price stability.

Monetarist policies are based on an observed close connection between rises in the money supply and subsequent rates of inflation. They assume that the real level of economic activity cannot be influenced (other than in the short-run) by government fiscal policy. Control of the money supply leads to price stability. Expansionary fiscal policy is likely to impose a serious constraint on the ability of the authorities to control the supply of money and consequently the increase the likelihood of inflation. A budget deficit may be financed by borrowing from the domestic private sector, from the central bank, or from abroad. If the government borrows from the central bank it increases the money supply. There may also be a monetary expansion if they borrow from abroad.[2] If they borrow from the domestic private sector then this may increase the rate of interest and 'crowd out' some investment expenditure. These monetary effects of fiscal policy are often ignored by extreme Keynesians, who concentrate on the direct expenditure effects of fiscal policy. Monetarists argue that the importance of fiscal policy is derived from the financial consequences of such a policy for the money supply.

Since monetarists argue that government macroeconomic policy cannot have a long-run effect on economic activity, and hence employment levels, they do not favour government fiscal intervention to foster full-employment. In this sense monetarist policies are not compatible with full employment (i.e. all workers being employed) since they are prepared to accept a natural level of unemployment. However, monetarist policies can be used in connection with other policies to achieve, simultaneously, price stability and full employment. Therefore in this alternative view the second statement is also invalid.

[2] If the government sells gilt-edged stock to non-residents and operates a fixed exchange rate policy, it will increase the supply of sterling on the foreign exchange market to meet the increased demand, so the supply of money will increase.

Although the objectives of government policy are fairly well defined, the means to achieve them are the subject of considerable differences of opinion among economists. On the one hand, there is a group who advocate a minimum of government intervention and the adoption of a set of fixed rules which should be publicised fully. On the other hand, there is another group who claim that recent fluctuations in economic activity, employment and inflation could have been mimimised with additional government intervention.

If the government choses a policy of minimum intervention, then the market system must be relied upon to respond to changes in the pattern of demand, technology, external factors, or any other variable affecting the allocation of resources and the distribution of goods. The market system will work providing that prices respond quickly to eliminate disequilibrium.

The interventionists argue that prices in the real world are fairly rigid. Manufacturers do not like to cut the prices of their products when demand falls. Similarly, workers do not usually accept reduced nominal wages when there is an excess - supply of labour. The existence of a national or industry-negotiated minimum wage for labour and the operation of a price code for products, which only allows price rises if costs increase, both provide evidence in the U.K. for such rigidities in the short-run. Thus, to eliminate excess-demand or excess-supply requires direct government action on the level of aggregate expenditure.

Although most western developed economies pursue active macro-economic policies based on Keynesian analysis, there are a number of practical problems associated with their use. Firstly, the government should be able to diagnose the current state of the economy before determining their optimal strategy. This is not an easy task. Data becomes available only after a time lag, and even if one or two observations suggest a deviation from normality, it may not be absolutely clear whether or not these are due to some chance factors which will not recur. Once the diagnosis is made the appropriate policy must be determined. This requires not only a qualitative decision (e.g. expand the money supply) but also quantitative and temporal choices (how much to expand the money supply and when and for how long). These decisions are based on highly imperfect information of how the macroeconomic variables interrelate, and are likely, therefore, to be taken with a great deal of uncertaintly as to their probable effects. There is also the problem of a time-lag between the instigation of a policy change and its resulting effects on macro-economic variables. This lag may be from one month for prices to respond to a cut in indirect taxes, to three or four years for an increase in the money supply to work through on to the price level.

The non-interventionists, mainly associated with the monetarist school, claim that demand-management policies have ofteen been counter productive. Frequent changes in monetary and fiscal policy may accentuate instability in the economy rather than reduce it. It is claimed that this instability has contributed towards a lack of investment, and consequent low rate of growth in the U.K. since the war. They recommend a policy of adopting a constant rate of growth of the money supply. This implies a neutral balance between government expenditure and taxation and presumes a method of financing a budget deficit which is consistent with the monetary rule.

Such monetary rules have recently found favour with the U.K. government. Although there is not much evidence to evaluate this policy, it seems to be more acceptable to such international bodies as the I.M.F. There are problems associated with its implementation. Firstly, since there are several alternative definitions of money, it may not be clear which should be the subject of control, especially when there are large differences in the rate of growth of alternatively defined versions of the money supply. Secondly, it is argued that a fixed rate of growth of money will generate unemployment, especially if a high rate of inflation is presently being experienced. However, this is not only an argument against fixed monetary rules, since any policy designed to reduce inflation will generate unemployment. Thirdly, it is claimed that even if monetary targets are met, the high level of foreign trade in the U.K. would introduce instabilities in the domestic economy arising from world-wide fluctuations in the level of economic activity.

In conclusion, the debate between fixed rules versus discretionary macroeconomic policy has not been resolved completely. It is true to say that many economists have realised the limitations of fine tuning the economy. It seems we must wait for the results of the current 'monetary targets' policy to be assessed before evaluating the merits of the respective theories.

In the simple Keynesian-cross model of income determination, changes in the level of investment cause fluctuations in the level of economic activity. The size of this effect is determined by the investment multiplier, which is defined as the ratio of a change in income to the change in investment which brought it about. Its value is given by the reciprocal of the marginal propensity to save (mps). Fig. 31 shows that the effect of a rise in investment from I_1 to I_2 is to raise income from Y_1 to Y_2, other variables remaining constant.

As an example suppose the level of savings is given by the following equation:
$$S = -50 + \tfrac{1}{4}Y$$

If investment is initially at a level of 100, then the equilibrium level of income may be determined by setting $I = S$.

Therefore $100 = -50 + \tfrac{1}{4}Y$

    or $\tfrac{1}{4}Y = 150$

which implies $Y = 600$

Now, if investment rises to a level of 150, then at the income level of 600, savings will be less than investment and so income will rise.

Again, we may calculate the new equilibrium value by setting $I = S$

    $150 = -50 + \tfrac{1}{4}Y$

Fig. 31

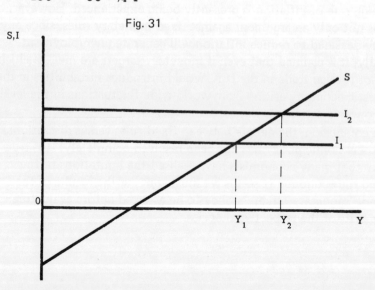

Therefore   ¼Y = 200
and   Y   = 800

So an increase in investment of 50 has generated an increase in income of 200. The investment multiplier is therefore $\frac{200}{50} = 4$.

Alternatively, noting the mps equals ¼, we can find the multiplier directly to be 4. Then given an increase in the investment of 50, we can predict that income will rise by 200 (the multiplier times the increase in investment, 4×50). Although there are a number of other important factors affecting both the size of the multiplier and changes in the level of income, we have established that fluctuations in investment can cause economic instability.

The reasons why the level of investment expenditure is more volatile than other types of expenditure is attributable to several factors. The accelerator model provides one such justification. Here the assumption of a fixed capital - output ratio (v) leads to the assumption that investment expenditure is related to changes in output.

$$\text{If } \frac{K_t}{Y_t} = v$$

and investment is defined as the change in the capital stock, then

$$I_t = K_t - K_{t-1}$$
$$\therefore \quad I_t = vY_t - vY_{t-1}$$
$$\therefore \quad I_t = v\Delta Y_t$$

where $\Delta Y_t = Y_t - Y_{t-1}$

So if $v = 4$, an increase in income of 100 will raise investment by 400. If output increases in response to some exogenous change (e.g. a rise in exports) then firms will increase their capital stock, in order to meet the higher demand. Then through the multiplier, this increase in investment will cause income to rise even further. As expenditure rises, firms will increase their investment demands yet again to maintain the capital - output ratio. Eventually capacity constraints being the process to an end. This inter-relationship between the multiplier and the accelerator then provides one explanation of the trade cycle.

A second important reason for the volatility of investment expenditure arises from the uncertainties associated with potential profits firms anticipate. Expectations of optimism/pessimism about future sales may considerably modify firms investment behaviour. Also, variations in either the cost of capital equipment or the rate of interest can be expected to have some effect. The output of capital goods in any one year is only a small proportion of the total capital stock. So in times of high demand it is quite possible that shortages and bottlenecks will develop. These will lead to longer delivery dates on orders and/or higher prices, which will eventually stem the increase in investment. If firms want to invest they must obtain the necessary funds. A large proportion is usually met from undistributed profits, but some has to be borrowed. When firms plan to increase investment expenditure they will increase the demand for loans, which may raise their borrowing costs. This will be more important for long-lived projects than for short-term ones.

In conclusion, the interaction between changes in determining expenditure and economic activity leads to some difficulty in determining a causal pattern. Not only do investment fluctuations cause variations in the level of national incomes, but also changes in income cause the level of investment to alter. Thus it is true to say that the volatility of investment causes instability, but it is also true that economic instability contributes towards the volatility of investment.

Answer 52   Economic Growth   Question page 14

Investment plays a dual role in the growth process. Firstly, it is an injection into the circular flow. Changes in the level of investment have multiplier effects on income and expenditure. Over time, the growth of investment expenditure therefore contributes towards the growth of aggregate demand. Secondly, investment expenditure raises the stock of capital, increasing the productive capacity of the economy. Consequently the growth of aggregate supply also depends on the growth of investment expenditure.

Economic growth is concerned with changes in the full employment level of real national income per capita. To achieve stable growth a balanced increase in both demand and supply is required. An economy on a stable growth path is always in equilibrium at the full employment level. This means that planned expenditure at constant prices will always be equal to the level of output generated at full employment. If planned expenditure grows at a faster rate than capacity, then inflation will emerge. If it grows at a slower rate the result will be unemployment.

To see the role of investment, consider a simple model of economic growth. Suppose the incremental capital output ratio (ICOR) is a fixed value v, i.e. $I = vDZ$, where I is the change in the capital stock (investment) and DZ is the change in the level of output it is able to produce. So if $v = 4$, an extra £100 of investment will enable output to rise by 25. Then the change in productive capacity can be related to investment:

$$DZ = \frac{I}{v}$$

On the demand side, the investment multiplier determines the effect on aggregate expenditure of an increase in investment. If DY represents the change in income, DI the change in investment, and MPS is the marginal propensity to save then :

$$\frac{DY}{DI} = \frac{1}{MPS} \quad \text{or} \quad DY = \frac{DI}{MPS}$$

If MPS = 1/5, and DI = £5, then aggregate income rises by £25. For balanced growth we require supply and demand to increase by the same amount i.e. $DY = DZ$

Therefore $\quad \dfrac{I}{v} = \dfrac{DI}{MPS}$

On rearranging, we obtain a rate of growth of investment (G_i) as follows:

$$G_i = \frac{DI}{I} = \frac{MPS}{v}$$

If the MPS is 1/5 and the incremental capital-output ratio is 4, the rate of growth for economic stability is

$$G_i = \frac{1}{5} \div 4 = \frac{1}{20} = 5\%$$

It should be noted that when investment grows at a constant rate then, given constant returns to scale, other inputs must also be increasing at the same rate. In the case of labour this may present problems, for there is no reason why the rate of growth of labour supply (known as the natural rate of growth G_L) should equal the required rate for stable growth (the warranted rate determined above, G_i).

The process of economic development depends on several factors: population, natural resources, capital formation and the rate of technical change. The developing countries can copy the advanced technology of the developed nations, and may also have abundant natural resources and an excess supply of labour. Thus the binding constraint on their rate of growth is likely to be their ability to acquire capital.

For many less developed nations there exists a classic problem of undersaving. Income levels are so low that practically all of it has to be spent on current consumption goods in order to survive. Thus little savings are generated within the domestic economy. In addition political instability or an underdeveloped financial system, may mean much of the limited savings are in fact hoarded rather than saved (ie. not recirculated within the financial system as loanable funds.) With domestic savings unable to finance sufficient investment in advanced technology the less-developed nations may turn abroad, to obtain foreign sources of capital. These are mainly derived as aid from international economic organisations (such as the World Bank and the European Development Fund), or individual governments. Not all foreign aid is beneficial, however, for various 'strings' may be attached, such as the requirement that a proportion of the aid must be spent on goods from the lending country, with the consequent commitment to purchase spare parts etc. It is also claimed that foreign aid may reduce incentives of workers, or be associated with political pressure.

For these reasons the acquisition of funds to finance investment is difficult for the less developed nations. Therefore it is very important that they acquire the most appropriate type of equipment to use with their other existing factors of production.

If the less - developed nations copy advanced techniques it does not follow that their industries will operate efficiently. There are two main reasons for this. Firstly, even using advanced technology, they may still produce the wrong commodity at the wrong place at the wrong time (lack of demand). This is an example of allocative inefficiency, which is a problem that may only be solved by improving the entrepreneurial abilities, or planning system of the developing nation. A second source of inefficiency may be due to different cultural or educational backgrounds. For example key executives in a developing economy may be appointed on a 'class', 'family' or wealth basis, rather than on ability, or workers using complex machinery may be unable to perform simple calculations or read manuals. This may seriously reduce productivity compared to similar techniques used elsewhere. This problem is known as X-inefficiency.

To some extent the developing nations are caught in a cleft stick. They do not have sufficient capital to emulate the more advanced economies' technological achievements. Even if they succeed in copying some sophisticated techniques, these usually generate lower income than anticipated because of allocative and X-inefficiency. If they do not copy advanced techniques they maintain low rates of growth using traditional inefficient methods.

One possible solution, suggested by Dr. Schumacher, is to introduce 'intermediate technology'. Less complex methods of production would probably involve a lower level of X-inefficiency. Moreover, as less capital is required relative to labour, it may generate a much needed boost to employment. This process is inevitably slow, given the constraints on funds, but it appears to be the most acceptable route towards economic development. Since the above quotation does not allow the possibility of using intermediate technology for economic development, we must disagree with the conclusion that either traditional inefficient methods or sophisticated techniques have to be used.

Answer 54   **Income Distribution**   **Question page 14**

The distribution of income in the U.K. has remained relatively stable for a number of years, despite government attempts to reduce the degree of inequality. This has lead some economists to suggest new measures to deal with the problem of poverty. Two such policies are the negative income tax (NIT), and the social dividend (SD). Both use the tax system as the basis for redistribution.

The NIT system has four main features: a basis of assessment of income and needs; a minimum guaranteed income; rates of positive and negative taxation; and at least one tax threshold. Fig. 32 indicates how a simplified version could operate to reduce the degree of inequality in pre-tax incomes. For a given gross income, measured along the horizontal axis, the kinked line CDE indicates the associated income after tax, measured on the vertical axis. OB is the single tax threshold. Gross income earners receiving less than

OB are given a transfer payment equal to the vertical difference between OD and CD, and are therefore beneficiaries under the scheme. Those earning in excess of OB then pay taxes equal to the vertical distance between DA and DE and are therefore net contributors towards the scheme.

Clearly the greater the degree of redistribution attempted, the flatter will be CD. In the limiting case a negative tax rate of 100% would maintain all incomes at a minimum level of OB. Then, no matter how much the worker earned below OB, his post-tax income

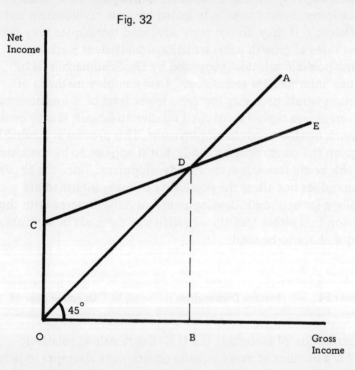

Fig. 32

would always be made up to OB. If the negative tax rate is less than 100% it may still contribute towards the 'poverty trap' where low income earners who receive a pay rise lose a large proportion via the associated reduction in means-tested transfer payments.

The disincentive effect of high marginal tax rates at low income levels has not been empirically verified. It may seem likely that workers will prefer not to work longer hours when much of their additional pay is clawed back by taxation, but this cannot be justified at present. One other incentive effect of NIT may concern its possible abuse by employers. If firms know that workers are indifferent between wage income and transfer payments then there is an incentive for them to reduce their pay offers, relying on the government to make good the short fall in income.

The SD scheme involves the payment of a minimum income to all tax units, and to classify all income (including this transfer) as taxable. Fig. 33 illustrates how this policy could operate. OB represents the size of the social dividend. As income rises, a constant proportion is assumed to be paid in taxes. The slope of the line BCD

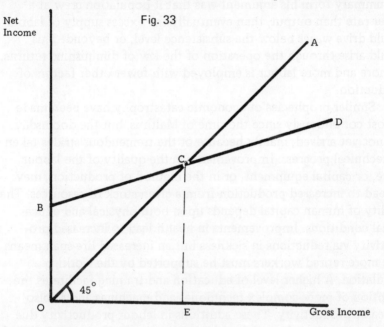

Fig. 33

indicates the tax rate. Below the income level OB, the social dividend exceeds the tax paid, and the tax unit is a beneficiary under the scheme. Above this income level the tax paid exceeds the social dividend and the unit becomes a net contributor towards the scheme. The main problem with this scheme is that with a fairly high SD, the tax rate required to finance it may be extremely high.

Again there is an argument concerning the potential effects of this policy. There may be little encouragement for individuals to work harder when it is known that a high proportion of their resulting rise in income will be taken in taxation. However, the disincentive effect may be less for the SD than for the NIT proposal. With the SD scheme the tax rate is likely to be less than the implied tax rate under NIT for low incomes. Thus a given increase in gross income will represent a greater net addition to income under the SD than NIT systems. For higher income earners the results may be reversed, so that no general overall conclusion can be drawn.

The rate of economic growth depends on several factors, but its relationship with the growth of population has been a central issue of discussion for many years dating back to Thomas Malthus' book "An Essay on the Principle of Population" published in 1798. In summary form his argument was that if population grew at a faster rate than output, then eventually the excess supply of labour would drive wages below the subsistence level, or beyond. This would arise through the operation of the law of diminishing returns, as more and more labour is employed with fewer other factors of production.

Similar prophecies of economic catastrophy have been made almost continuously since the time of Malthus, but the doomsday has not yet arrived, mainly because of the tremendous strides taken by technical progress. Improvements in the quality of the labour force, or capital equipment, or in the method of production, may all lead to increased production from a given stock of resources. The quality of human capital depends upon both physical and educational conditions. Improvements in health lead to increased productivity via reductions in sickness but an increased life-span means that more retired workers must be supported by the working population. A higher level of education and training facilitates the adoption of more complex techniques and machines and so also increases productivity. These additions in labour productivity due to an improved quality of the labour force may offset the effects of diminishing returns due to the increased quantity of labour.

As the process of economic growth and development proceeds, there is likely to be an effect on population growth. In a less developed country, birth rates and death rates are high, and productivity is low. The first demographic change introduced by an increase in the standard of living is a reduction in the death rate. Increased medical facilities also reduce infant mortality, and so the rate of population growth accelerates. As long as this is accompanied by a rapid growth in demand, and also given investment is sufficient to increase labour productivity, per capital income rises. After a period, the increased standard of living causes a fall in the birth rate. The final position of stability then, is associated with low birth- and death rates and high productivity. The complete process has occurred in all developed economies so far.

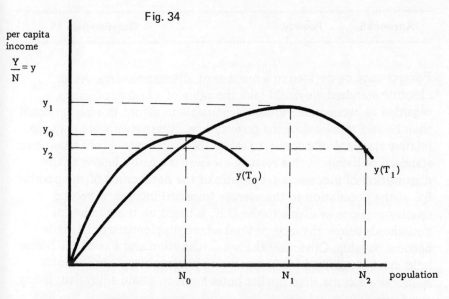

Fig. 34

The most difficult phase of this demographic transition from a less developed to a developed economy occurs when the rate of population increase is at a maximum. Then there is a chance that the rate of balanced growth may become less than this natural rate of increase of the population. [1] That is, investment is growing at a slow rate and so both aggregate demand andssupply cannot keep pace with population increases, thus per capita incomes will fall.

This may be illustrated graphically. Fig. 34 denotes an economically optimal population of N_0 at time T_0. The per capita level of income y_0 represents the maximum that can be produced with existing resources and techniques i.e. the maximum of the per capita short-run production function $y(T_0)$. At a population below N_0 the existing stock of other resources has too little labour to be combined with efficiently. If the population were greater than N_0, diminishing returns would ensure a lower per capita income. As technical progress and investment occur, the optimal population increases so that a t time T_1, it has risen to N_1, where the maximum of the new per capita production function is y_1. If during this period the actual population rises from N_0 to N_2, then per capita income will fall to y_2. In this situation the only way to achieve a higher standard of living is to pursue policies designed to reduce the rate of population growth.

1. See the answer to Q.52. for further discussion of the relationship between the natural and balanced rates of growth.

Poverty may be defined in a number of alternative ways. As an absolute standard we could take the value of a basket of goods regarded as necessities. Households unable to afford this basket could then be said to lie below the poverty line. Alternatively we may use a relative standard of poverty to relate the problem to a generally rising standard of living. Such a relative measure is usually linked to the distribution of income, e.g. the ratio of the net income of the poorest 5% of the population to the average (median) income. A second relative measure available to the U.K. is based on the number of households below the income level where supplementary benefits become payable. Obviously the age distribution and size of the household must be allowed for in measuring poverty—larger households need more income than smaller households to attain equivalent living standards.

Low pay in employment is one important factor determining low income. However, the unemployed and those not currently part of the working population (the old, the young and the sick) may have to rely solely on social security for their needs, so that their income may fall below the poverty line for reasons not associated with low pay. The original aim of the National Insurance system was to provide a level of benefit at least equal to the poverty line but it has not been successful in so doing. Of course, low paid workers are also entitled to various benefits, means-tested or otherwise (e.g. Family Income Supplements, rent and rate rebates in the U.K.). The problem of poverty associated with low pay may therefore be resolved either by increasing the income from employment or by increasing social security provisions. Since 1971 the latter method has been adopted in the U.K. with the development of the Family Income Supplement, which is a form of Negative Income Tax. In this answer we are concerned with with the possible merits of the former.

Low pay in employment may be due either to pure market forces (where demand for and supply of labour give rise to a low level of wages) or to monopsonistic behaviour by a large firm (where the firm exploits its advantage of being the sole buyer of labour). Clearly the establishment of a national minimum wage at or below existing wage levels will have no effect, therefore let us consider whether its imposition above existing levels can eliminate poverty due to low pay. Consider the competitive labour market represented in Fig. 35. D_L and S_L represent the demand for and supply of labour.

In equilibrium the wage rate and level of employment are W_0 and L_0 respectively. If a minimum wage of W_1 is established above W_0 in an attempt to raise wages we can see that this objective is achieved but not without costs. Firms must now pay the minimum wage W_1 to hire any quantity of labour up to L_2. Thus the portion of the labour supply curve below L_2 (i.e. YZ) is replaced by the horizontal line emanating from W_1. Employment (L_1) is determined by the inter-section of this new labour supply curve with the demand curve. Employment has therefore been reduced from L_0 to L_1 by the imposition of the minimum wage. Although those in employment now receive higher wages, which may alleviate their poverty problem, there is some increase in unemployment. If existing social security provisions are inadequate then the problem of poverty may well be exacerbated.

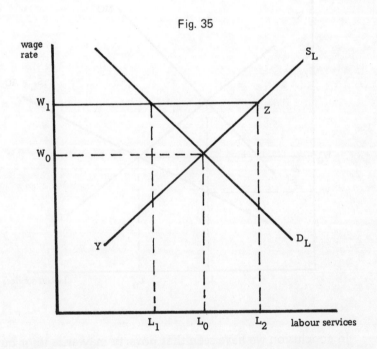

Fig. 35

A different result may emerge when low pay is caused by mono-polistic behavious on the part of a large firm. This situation is shown in Fig. 36. D_L and S_L again represent labour demand and supply curves. The supply curve is also the average cost (AC) of labour to the firm. Associated with this average cost curve is a marginal cost curve (MC). This shows the marginal increase in labour costs incurred by paying the higher wage (required to attract additional labour services) to all workers. The profit-maximising firm then determines the level of employment (L_1) by equating MC with D_L. To induce a labour supply equal to L_1 the firm need only offer a wage of W_1. If a minimum wage of W_0 is established then the AC and MC of labour are altered. Both are now constant at W_0 until point Z is reached. Under these conditions the firm will increase employment to L_0. Thus if there are monopsonistic conditions prevailing then the imposition of a minimum wage can not only increase the pay of those initially in employment, but also increase the level of employment in the industry. This argument then provides a justification for imposing minimum wages only in suitable industries.

Fig. 36

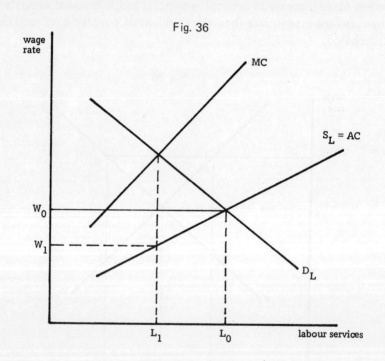

In conclusion we have seen that poverty may arise in or out of employment. Low pay in employment is only one facet of the problem. The establishment of a national minimum wage above existing levels will reduce employment in competitive labour markets and increase employment in monosonistic situations only.

Many ores and fossilized fuels are non-renewable, i.e. when existing stocks of these commodities are exhausted the world economy will have to manage without them. Although additional exploration and development may enlarge the available sources, there exists some finite stock which is in fixed supply. The demand for such resources takes the form of a flow rather than a stock—only a fraction of the total stock of oil, for example, is used in any one year. Thus even if the total stock of a resource is fixed the question of how the market will allocate its use over time (i.e. the flow decision) remains.

If the extraction cost of the resource is low then an upper limit to its rate of use may be derived. The owners of the resource have to decide on the optimum rate of production per period, which also determines the amount of the resource to be conserved for future use. The greater the amount of the resource supplied now, the lower the present price will be. Also, higher prices may be induced following the contraction of the available future stock. This assumes, of course, a stable demand over time. A capital gain will thus be expected by owners who conserve the resource. The expected size of this capital gain is equal to the anticipated rate of increase in the price of the resource. Owners of the resource who sell now receive current revenue, which could be lent at the current rate of interest. The relative profitability of production compared with conserving stocks depends on the relative sizes of the expected capital gain and the rate of interest.

Suppose the expected capital gain exceeded the current interest rate. It would pay the owners of the resource to reduce present production and conserve more stocks, since the interest lost is more than compensated for by the capital gain. Thus the present price of the resource would increase and expected future prices will fall. Eventually the expected capital gain would become equal to (or less than) the current interest rate. In this situation the rate of use of the scarce resource would gradually decline bringing with it a continuous rise in its price.

As mentioned earlier this argument assumes low extraction costs and a stable demand curve over time. In practice these assumptions may not be met. Firstly, if marginal extraction costs are high relative to the current price of the resource then there may be no incentive to deplete stocks (i.e. increase current supply) at a rate fast enough to generate a capital gain on conserved stocks equal to the rate of interest. The price rise would then be more gradual, as would the decline in the rate of use of the scarce resource. Secondly demand conditions may not remain constant. Economic growth may shift the demand curve outwards over time. This may temporarily increase its rate of use and stimulate even faster price increases. Alternatively, as the present price of the resource increases, the search for substitutes (or the possibility of recycling) will accelerate. If successful this will reduce the demand for the resource lowering both its price and rate of use.

The market system thus responds to the depletion of a non-renewable resource by a gradual reduction in its use, encouraged by a continuous price rise, the percentage increase in price being generally limited by the rate of interest. Shifts in demand conditions caused by economic growth or the development of substitutes may also be expected to affect both its current price and rate of use.

Appendix 1

Question 1

The diagram shows some of an individual's indifference curves for two goods, food - purchased in kilos, and drink - purchased in litres. The price of food is £2 per kilo and drink costs 50p. per litre. Initially the individual's expenditure is £20 per week.

a) Find the quantity of each good purchased by the individual if he maximises utility.

b) Promotion enables him to raise his expenditure to £30 per week. How does this affect his purchases?

c) Expenditure is maintained at £30 per week, and food subsidies are introduced, halving the price of food but leaving the price of drink unchanged. What quantities should he purchase?

d) Indicate how a demand schedule for food could be constructed from the indifference curves if the individual's expenditure, preferences, and the price of drink remained constant.

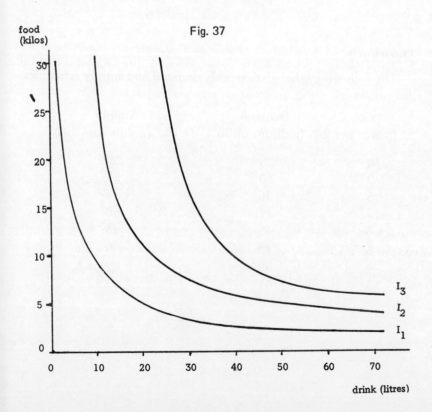

Fig. 37

Question 2

Demand and supply schedules for a particular commodity are available as follows:

Price (£)	Demand (millions per week)	Supply (millions per week)
15	50	140
14	60	120
13	70	100
12	80	80
11	90	60
10	100	40

a) Find the equilibrium price and quantity traded.

b) Suppose the government imposes a tax of £3 per unit on the commodity. Find the new equilibrium price and quantity traded.

c) By how much has producer's total revenue (net of tax) been altered?

Question 3

The following table gives weekly demand and supply schedules for potatoes.

Price (pence per lb)	Demand (millions of lbs.)	Supply (millions of lbs.)
10	23	59
9	30	57
8	36	54
7	41	50
6	45	45
5	48	39
4	50	32
3	51	25

a) Find the equilibrium price and quantity traded.
b) Examine the effects of imposing a maximum price of
   (i) 5p. per lb. (ii) 7p. per lb.
c) If the government guaranteed potato suppliers a price of 7p. per lb., what quantity would it have to purchase to maintain this price?
d) If alternatively, the government bought all potatoes on offer at 7p. per lb., what price would it have to charge consumers to dispose of this quantity?
e) Calculate the operating costs to the government of operating the schemes outlined in (c) and (d) above.

Question 4

The weekly market demand for a good is as follows:

Price (pence)	Quantity demanded (units)
10	250
9	350
8	550
7	600
6	700
5	1000
4	1500

a) Calculate the price elasticity of demand for:
   (i)   a price fall from 10p. to 9p.
   (ii) a price rise from 5p. to 6p.
b)   If the price is increased from 10p. to 11p. and the elasticity of demand is−6, find the quantity demanded at the higher price.
c) If the price is lowered from 4p. to 3p. and the elasticity of demand is −10, find the quantity demanded at the lower price.
d) If average real incomes rise by 10%, the quantity demanded at each price increases by 100 units. Calculate the income elasticity of demand when the market price is
   (i)   10p. per lb.
   (ii) 4p. per lb.

Question 5

The following information on total costs and output for a particular firm is available:

Production (units per week)	Total cost (£)
4	2800
5	3300
6	3900
7	4550
8	5400
9	6300
10	7500

Fixed costs are £500

a) Define 'marginal cost' and 'average cost' and calculate their values over the given range of production.

b) If the market price is given at £875, find the profit-maximising level of output (to the nearest whole unit of production).

c) If the market in which this firm operates is perfectly competitive and all firms have the same costs (as above), find the long-run market price.

d) Find the minimum price at which the firm will produce some output
    i) in the short-run
    ii) in the long-run.

Question 6

An engineer needs a generator for use over the next 5 years. He could purchase a reconditioned second-hand model costing £500, which will last 5 years if £50 a year is spent on repairs, and which will have no resale value at the end of the period. Alternatively, he could buy a new model costing £250 that would also last 5 years if a part costing £100 is replaced in 3 years time and have an end of period resale value of £750. Both types of generator perform equally well and their running costs are identical. If the cost of capital to the firm is 10%, which type of generator should be purchased?

Period (n)	0	1	2	3	4	5
Discount Factor (at 10%)	1	0.909	0.826	0.751	0.683	0.621

Question 7

An industry is composed of 50 firms, whose marginal costs (in £) are as follows:

Output (units)	10 firms like A	10 firms like B	15 firms like C	15 firms like D
1	2	4	6	8
2	4	6	8	10
3	6	8	10	12
4	8	10	12	14
5	10	12	14	16
6	12	14	16	18

a) Construct the supply schedule for the industry between prices of £2 and £12.

b) The industry demand schedule is as follows:

Price (£)	12	10	8	6	4	2
Quantity demanded (units)	75	95	115	135	155	175

Find the equilibrium price, the total industry output, and the output of each type of firm. Assume each firm is operating above the minimum of its average variable cost.

c) Following a fall in average income the demand schedule is now becomes:

Price (£)	12	10	8	6	4	2
Quantity demanded (Units)	10	30	50	65	85	115

Find the new equilibrium price, and the number of firms now engaged in production.

Question 8

A monopolist faces the following demand schedule:

Price (£)	20	18	16	14	12	10
Quantity demanded (units per week)	50	60	70	80	90	100

Output may only be produced in batches of 10.

a) Find the profit-maximising level of output, and the corresponding price he would set if his marginal costs were constant at

       (i) £5

      (ii) zero

b) Calculate the elasticity of demand at the output levels corresponding to (i) and (ii).

Question 9

The following schedule relates total output of commodity X to the input of labour services, which are only available in units of 100 hours.

Labour services (hrs. per week)	100	200	300	400	500	600	700
Output (units per week)	150	300	410	485	535	570	595

a) Construct the marginal physical product of labour schedule for commodity X.

b) If each unit of X sells for £5, and the current hourly wage is £2, how many hours of labour services should be hired?

c) Suppose the market price of X is £10, and the hourly wage is £8, how many hours of labour services should now be hired per week?

Question 10

Given the table below concerning a closed economy with no government sector:

a) Plot the relationship between consumption expenditure and National Income.

b) Calculate the value of the marginal propensity to consume.

c) Determine the size of the multiplier.

d) Find the average propensity to save when National Income is £200m.

National Income £m	Consumption of Expenditure £m
60	88.2
80	102.6
100	117.0
120	131.4
140	145.8
160	160.2
180	174.6
200	189.0
220	203.4
240	217.8

Question 11

The following relationships hold in a particular economy:

Consumers' expenditure is £2m. plus 4/5ths of personal disposable income.

Gross domestic fixed investment is £2.5m.

Firms retain 1/6th (before tax) of gross domestic income as retained profits.

Government expenditure is £3.0 m.

All income is taxed at 25%.

Exports are £1.5m.

Imports are 10% of gross domestic product.

There are no expenditure taxes and the aggregate price level is constant.

Calculate a) the equilibrium level of income
         b) the balance of trade
and   c) the budget surplus or deficit.

Question 12

A closed economy with no government sector exhibits the following relationship between consumption expenditure (C) and National Income (Y) :

$$C = £50 \text{ m.} + \tfrac{3}{4} Y$$

a)   What is the value of savings when Y = £200.
b)   If investment equals £100 m., find the equilibrium level of income.
c)   Calculate the value of the multiplier and hence deduce the effect on the equilibrium level of income if investment rises to £150 m.
d)   The consumption function now becomes:
$$C = £50 \text{ m.} + 4/5 \, Y$$

How are your answers to a), b) and c) affected?

Question 13

In the country of Imagecon, the following macroeconomic relationships are known:

$$C = 3 + \frac{4}{5} \, yd$$
$$I = 5$$
$$G = 8$$
$$T = tY$$
$$Y_d = Y - T$$

where: C is consumers' expenditure   (£m.)
       Y_d is disposable income   (£m.)
       I is gross investment   (£m.)
       G is government expenditure   (£m.)
       T is income tax revenue   (£m.)
       t is the tax rate   (%)
       Y is national income   (£m.)

a)   Calculate the equilibrium level of income in Imagecon when the tax rate is 25%.
b)   Given the full employment level of income is £50m. derive the required changes in
      (i)   government expenditure
and (ii)   the tax rate

to achieve equilibrium at full employment.

Question 14

The demand for money in a particular economy is determined as follows. The demand for active balance is one-third of annual money income. The demand for idle balances is related to the rate of interest according to the schedule:

interest rate (%)	0	2	4	6	8	10	12	14	16	18	20
demand for idle balances £m.	1500	1400	1300	1200	1100	1000	900	800	700	600	500

a) If annual money income is £2400m, and the money supply is £16000 m. find the equilibrium interest rate.

b) If annual money income is £300 m. and the government wishes to set the interest rate at 10%, what value should they choose for the money supply?

Question 15

Country A has sufficient resources to produce 100 units of commodity X, or 1,000 units of commodity Y, or any combination of X and Y provided that it forgoes 10 units of Y to produce 1 extra unit of X.

Country B can produce 500 units of X, or 1500 units of Y, or any combination of X and Y provided it forgoes 3 units of Y for each extra unit of X produced.

a) Show that both countries can gain from trade

b) Find the range of relative prices of X in terms of Y over which trade will actually take place.

Answers to numerical questions

Answer 1

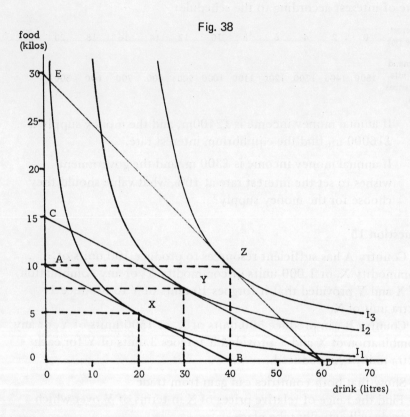

Fig. 38

a) The initial budget line is given by AB in Fig. 38 . It cuts the food axis at $\frac{£20}{£2}$ = 10 kilos, and the drinks axis at

$\frac{£20}{£0.50}$ = 40 litres. AB is tangential to indifference curve I_1 at

point X. The quantities purchased are <u>5 kilos</u> of food and <u>10 litres</u> of drink.

b) The new budget constraint is CD, parallel to AB. It cuts the food axis at $\dfrac{£30}{£2}$ = 15 kilos, and the drinks axis at $\dfrac{£30}{£0.50}$ = 60 litres. CD is tangential to indifference curve I_2 at Y, where 7½ kilos of food and 30 litres of drink are consumed.

c) ED is the new budget constraint. The intercept on the axis are $\dfrac{£30}{£1}$ = 30 kilos of food, and $\dfrac{£30}{£0.50}$ = 60 litres of drink respectively. ED is tangential to indifference curve I_3 at point Z. The quantities purchased are : 10 kilos of food and 40 litres of drink.

d) By varying the price of food the budget line may be made to rotate. The set of each associated point of tangency with an indifference curve will generate a price consumption curve. The demand schedule may be obtained from this curve by relating the quantity of food demanded to the price of food.

Answer 2

a) The equilibrium price is £12 and quantity traded is 80 million per week.

b) The imposition of a £3 per unit tax shifts the supply curve upwards by the full amount of the tax, since producers are only willing to supply the same quantities at £3 more than they were originally (in order to pay the tax). A portion of the new supply curve is given below, together with the original demand schedule.

Price (£)	Demand (millions per week)	Supply (millions per week)
15	50	80
14	60	60
13	70	40
12	80	-
11	90	-
10	100	-

The new equilibrium price is £14 and the quantity traded is 60 million per week.

c)   The industry's initial revenue was

$$£12 \times 80 \text{ m.} = £960 \text{ m.}$$

After tax the industry's revenue is

$$(£14 - £3) \times 60 \text{ m.} = £660 \text{ m.}$$

Therefore total revenue earned in the industry has fallen by
$£960$ m.– $£660$ m. = $£300$ m.

Answer 3

a)   The equilibrium price is 6p. per lb. and the quantity traded
is 45 m. lbs.

b)   (i) At a price of 5p. demand (48 m. lbs.) exceeds supply
(39 m. lbs.). Since 5p. is the maximum price we would expect
this situation of excess-demand to lead to the emergence of
non-price competition among consumers (e.g. queuing,
rationing) or even a black market.

(ii) A maximum price set above the equilibrium price has no
effect, since the original equilibrium price and quantity are
still attainable.

c)   At a price of 7p, supply exceeds demand by 50 m. lbs —
41 m. lbs. = 9 m. lbs. This is the quantity which the government must purchase to maintain its guaranteed price of 7p.

d)   Supply equals 50 m.lbs. at 7p. To sell 50 m.lbs. to consumers
the government must set a price of 4p.

e)   The costs of operating these schemes are as follows: to
maintain the guaranteed price at 7p. requires the purchase of
9 m.lbs. If we ignore storage and disposal costs then this
gives a total operating cost of 7p. x 9 m = £630,000.

To buy 50 m.lbs. at 7p. and sell them at 4p. gives a total cost
of (7p.– 4p.) x 50 m.   =   £1,500,000

Thus the first alternative is cheaper.

Answer 4

a) Price elasticity of demand (e) is defined as:

$$e = \frac{\text{percentage change in quantity demanded}}{\text{percentage change in price}}$$

$$= \frac{\frac{\Delta Q}{Q} \times 100\%}{\frac{\Delta P}{P} \times 100\%} = \frac{\Delta Q}{\Delta P} \cdot \frac{P}{Q}$$

where ΔQ is the change in quantity demanded

ΔP is the change in price

and P and Q are the original price and quantity

(i) $P = 10$ $Q = 250$ $\Delta P = -1$ $\Delta Q = 100$

$$\therefore e = \frac{100}{-1} \cdot \frac{10}{250} = \underline{-4}$$

(ii) $P = 5$ $Q = 1000$ $\Delta P = 1$ $\Delta Q = -300$

$$\therefore e = \frac{-300}{1} \cdot \frac{5}{1000} = \underline{-1.5}$$

b) $e = -6$ $P = 10$ $Q = 250$ $\Delta P = 1$

$$\therefore -6 = \frac{\Delta Q}{1} \cdot \frac{10}{250}$$

$$\therefore \Delta Q = -150$$

$\therefore$ new quantity purchased $= 250 - 150$

$$= \underline{100}$$

This is the level of demand when $P = 11$

c) $e = -10$ $P = 4$ $Q = 1500$ $\Delta P = -1$

$$\therefore -10 = \frac{\Delta Q}{-1} \cdot \frac{4}{1500}$$

$$\therefore \Delta Q = 3,750$$

$\therefore$ new quantity purchased $= 1500 + 3,750$

$$= \underline{5250}$$

This is the quantity demanded at a price of 3p.

N.B. There are several alternative definitions of price elasticity. Point elasticity measures the elasticity at a single point on the demand curve and requires knowledge of the slope of the demand curve. Arc elasticity may be derived from the demand schedule and is a measure of the <u>average</u> price elasticity over the range. There are several versions of this measure. The one employed here is quite common. Sometimes the initial price and quantity in the formula are replaced by their average values over the interval chosen, or even their final values.

d)   Income elasticity of demand (n) may be defined as

$$n = \frac{\text{percentage change in quantity demanded}}{\text{percentage change in income}}$$

$$n = \frac{\dfrac{\Delta Q}{Q} \times 100\%}{\dfrac{\Delta Y}{Y} \times 100\%}$$

The percentage rise in income is 10%

(i)   P = 10   Q = 250 ΔQ = 100

$$\therefore \ n = \frac{\dfrac{100}{250} \times 100\%}{10\%} = 4$$

This is the income elasticity of demand when P = 10

(ii)   P = 4   Q = 1500 ΔQ = 100

$$n = \frac{\dfrac{100}{1500} \times 100\%}{10\%} = \frac{2}{3}$$

This is the income elasticity of demand when P = 4

Answer 5

(a)   Marginal cost (MC) may be defined as the increase in total cost incurred by producing an additional unit of output.

Average cost (AC) may be defined as total cost divided by the number of units of output produced.

Using these definitions and the given data we may construct the following schedules

Production (units per week)	Total Cost (£)	Average Cost (£)	Marginal Cost (£)
4	2800	700	500
5	3300	660	600
6	3900	650	650
7	4550	650	850
8	5400	675	900
9	6300	700	1200
10	7500	750	—

(b)   The firm will increase production while price exceeds marginal cost, and reduce production if price is less than marginal cost. Since the given price is £875, the firm will produce 8 units. As a check, if the firm produced only 7 units it could produce one more unit profitably, as revenue would increase by £875 whereas costs would rise by only £850. If it produced 9 units it could profitably reduce output by one unit. Costs would fall by £900 which exceeds the revenue lost (£875). Therefore 8 units is the profit-maximising level of output.

(c)   In the long run, a perfectly competitive firm operates at the minimum point of its average cost curve. Thus the firm would produce either 6 or 7 units at an average cost of £650. Since no excess profits would be earned in the long-run, the market price would also be equal to £650.

(d)   (i) The short-run shut-down point occurs when price falls below the minimum of the average variable cost. Total variable costs are equal to total cost minus fixed costs. Average variable costs are obtained by dividing total variable costs by the level of output. Using the above data we can construct these cost schedules.

Production (units per week)	Variable Costs (£)	Average Variable Cost* (£)
4	2300	575
5	2800	560
6	3400	567
7	4050	579
8	4900	612
9	5800	644
10	7000	700

*calculated to nearest £.

The minimum value of average variable cost is £560, and this is, therefore, the minimum price at which the firm will produce in the short-run.

(ii) The long-run shut-down point arises when price falls below average total cost. From (c) the minimum value of average cost is £650, which is the long-run price at which the firm will stay in production.

Answer 6

As running costs are identical they may be ignored. The cash outflow associated with each type of generator must be discounted to find the present cost.

The calculation of the discounted cash flow is as follows :

Year	Discount factor	Reconditioned Model cash flow	present value	New Model cash flow	present value
		(£)	(£)	(£)	(£)
0	1	-500	0500	-1250	-1250
1	0.909	-50	-45		
2	0.826	-50	-41		
3	0.751	-50	-38	-100	-75
4	0.683	-50	-34		
5	0.621	-50	-31	+750	+466
			-689		-859

Since the present cost of the reconditioned generator is smaller, this is the type the engineer should buy.

Answer 7

a)   Each firm's marginal cost curve is its supply curve. To find the industry supply curve we aggregate output of each firm at given prices. These calculations are presented in the following schedule.

Price (£) (	Type A (10 firms)	Type B (10 firms)	Type C (15 firms)	Type D (15 firms)	Aggregate supply
2	10	0	0	0	10
4	20	10	0	0	30
6	30	20	15	0	65
8	40	30	30	15	115
10	50	40	45	30	165
12	60	50	60	45	215

b)   By inspection demand equals supply at a price of £8, which is the equilibrium price. The equilibrium quantity traded is 115.

Output of each type of firm can be read from the above table.

  10 type A firms each produce 4 units
  10 type B firms each produce 3 units
  15 type C firms each produce 2 units
  15 type D firms each produce 1 unit

c) From the new demand schedule and the above supply schedule the equilibrium price is £6, and the equilibrium quantity traded is 65. Output of each type of firm may again be obtained from the table in a) :

  10 type A firms each produce 3 units
  10 type B firms each produce 2 units
  15 type C firms each produce 1 unit
  15 type D firms cease production.

Therefore the number of firms still engaged in production is 35 (10 type A, 10 type B and 15 type C).

Answer 8

a)   The profit-maximising monopolist determines his output level by reference to his marginal cost and marginal revenue. The computation of the marginal revenue schedule is as follows.

Price (£)	Quantity demanded (units per week)	Total Revenue (£)	Marginal Revenue (£)
20	50	1000	8
18	60	1080	4
16	70	1120	0
14	80	1120	-4
12	90	1080	-8
10	100	1000	—

The monopolist will increase production only when it is profitable, i.e. only while the marginal revenue on the next batch of 10 exceeds its marginal cost.

(i)   Marginal cost is £5. Profit is maximised at an output level of 60. Producing an extra batch of 10 would add more to costs (£50) than revenue (£40). Similarly cutting production by 10 would reduce revenue (£80) by more than costs (£50).
    From the demand schedule the price he must set to sell 60 units is £18.

(ii)   Marginal cost is zero. Profit is maximised at an output level of either 70 or 80 (since marginal revenue is also zero between this range of output.
    From the demand schedule : if output is 70 the price he sets is £16 ; if output is 80 the price he sets is £14.

b)   To calculate the elasticity of demand between output levels of 60 and 70, and between 70 and 80 units, use the formula :

$$e = \frac{\Delta Q}{\Delta P} \cdot \frac{P}{Q}$$

(i) $Q = 60$ $P = 18$ $\Delta P = -2$ $\Delta Q = 10$

$$\therefore \quad e = \frac{10}{-2} \cdot \frac{18}{60} = -1.5$$

(ii) $Q = 70$ $P = 16$ $\Delta P = -2$ $\Delta Q = 10$

$$\therefore \quad e = \frac{10}{-2} \cdot \frac{16}{70} = -1.142$$

Answer 9

a) The marginal physical product of labour (MPP_L) is the physical increment to total output produced by one additional unit of labour services,

i.e. $MPP_L = \dfrac{\Delta Q}{\Delta L}$

where ΔQ is the change in output
and ΔL is the change in labour services.

This enables us to construct the schedule for the MPP_L from the given production schedule.

Labour services (hrs. per week)	100	200	300	400	500	600	700
MPP_L		1.50	1.10	0.75	0.50	0.35	0.15	—

b)   The profit-maximising competitive firm hires labour services until the value of the marginal product ($P \times MPP_L$) which is the generated increase in revenue, becomes insufficient to cover the increase in costs, which is the wage rate. Thus the firm hires labour until the MPP_L falls below the ratio of wages to prices

since   W = £2   and   P = £5

$\therefore \quad \dfrac{W}{P} = \dfrac{2}{5} = 0.4$

Therefore the firm will hire <u>500 man hours.</u>

c)   Now   W = £8   P = £10

$\therefore \quad \dfrac{W}{P} = \dfrac{8}{10} = 0.8$

Therefore the firm will hire <u>300 man hours.</u>

Answer 10

a)

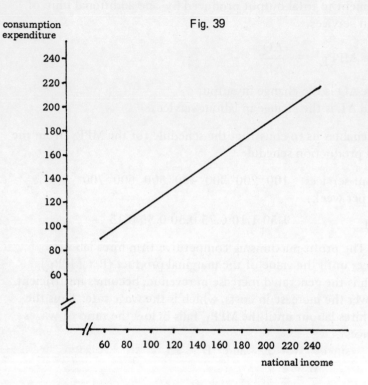

consumption expenditure

Fig. 39

national income

b)   The marginal propensity to consume is given by the ratio of a change in consumption to the change in income which induced it.

i.e.   M.P.C. = $\dfrac{\Delta C}{\Delta Y}$

As the consumption function is linear from a) we can choose any two points for the calculation. Using the first and last pair of observations :

ΔC = 217.8 - 88.2 = £129.6 m.
ΔY = 240 - 60   = £180 m.

∴ MPC   = $\dfrac{129.6}{180}$ = <u>0.72</u>

c) The multiplier (K) is given by the expression

$$K = \frac{1}{1 - MPC}$$

$$\therefore K = \frac{1}{1 - 0.72} = \frac{1}{.28} = \underline{3.57} \text{ approx.}$$

d)   The average propensity to save (APS) is equal to the ratio of savings to income.

when Y   = £200 m.   C = £189

$\therefore$ S = Y - C   = 200 - 189 = £11m.

$$\therefore APS = \frac{11}{200} = \underline{0.055}$$

Answer 11

a)   In equilibrium planned expenditure (E) equals national income (Y). Planned expenditure is the sum of consumption (C), investment (I), government expenditure (G) and exports (X) minus imports (F).

i.e.   Y = C + I + G + X - F   equation (i)

Now $C = 2 + \frac{4}{5} Ypd$ equation (ii)

where Ypd is personal disposable income, i.e. personal income after tax.
Since firms retain $\frac{1}{6}$ th of Y, personal income (Yp) is $\frac{5}{6}$ Y. All income is taxed at 25%, therefore

$$Ypd = \frac{3}{4} Yp = \frac{3}{4} \cdot \frac{5}{6} Y.$$

Substituting in equation (ii) yields :

$$C = 2 + \frac{4}{5} \cdot \frac{3}{4} \cdot \frac{5}{6} Y$$

$$\therefore C = 2 + \frac{1}{2} Y$$

Substituting the known values in equation (i) yields :

$$Y = 2 + \frac{1}{2}Y + 2.5 + 3.0 + 1.5 - \frac{1}{10}Y$$

$$\therefore Y = 9 + \frac{2}{5}Y$$

$$\therefore \frac{3}{5}Y = 9$$

therefore the equilibrium level of income is £15 m.

b) The Balance of trade (B) is equal to exports minus imports :

$$B = X - F$$

$$\therefore B = 1.5 - \frac{1}{10} \times 15 = 0$$

Therefore there is a <u>trade balance.</u>

c) The budget surplus (Z) is equal to tax revenue minus government expenditure

$$Z = T - G$$

$$\therefore Z = \frac{1}{4} \times 15 - 3 = £\frac{3}{4} m.$$

Answer 12

a) All income is either spent or saved

$$\therefore Y = C + S$$

$$S = Y - C$$

$$= Y - (50 - \frac{3}{4}Y)$$

$$\therefore S = -50 + \frac{1}{4}Y$$

when $Y = £200$ m

$$S = -50 + \frac{1}{4} \; 200 = 0$$

b)   In equilibrium aggregate planned expenditure equals
income.

$\therefore$ $Y = C + 1$

$\therefore$ $Y = 50 + \dfrac{3}{4} Y + 100$

$\therefore$ $(1-\dfrac{3}{4}) Y = 150$

$\therefore$ $Y \qquad = 4 \times 150 = $ £600 m.

c)   The multiplier (K) is given by

$$K = \frac{\Delta Y}{\Delta I} = \frac{1}{1 - MPC}$$

where ΔY is the change in income
ΔI is the change in investment

and MPC is the marginal propensity to consume

$\therefore$ $K = \dfrac{1}{1 - ¾} = \underline{4}$

$\therefore$ $\Delta Y = 4 \Delta I$

$\Delta I = 150 - 100 = 50$

$\therefore$ $\Delta Y = 4 \times 50 = $ £200 m

Hence the new level of income in equilibrium is

$600 + 200 = $ £800 m

d)   Repeating the calculations with the new relationship:

$$S = -50 + \frac{1}{5} Y$$

when $Y = 200$

$$S = -50 + \frac{1}{5} \times 200 = - £10 \ m$$

In equilibrium

$Y = C + I$

$\therefore$ $Y = 50 + \dfrac{4}{5} Y + 100$

$$\therefore \ (1 - \frac{4}{5})Y \ = \ 150$$

$$\therefore \ Y = 5 \times 150 \ = \ \underline{£750 \ m}$$

The multiplier $K \ = \ \dfrac{1}{1 - \dfrac{4}{5}} = \ \underline{5}$

$$\therefore \ \Delta Y \ = \ 5 \ \Delta I$$

$$= \ 5 \times 50 = \ £250m$$

$\therefore$ the new equilibrium level of income is

$$250 + 750 \ = \ \underline{£1000 \ m}$$

Answer 13

a)   In equilibrium planned expenditure (E) equals national income (Y). Planned expenditure is the sum of consumption (C) plus investment (I) plus government expenditure (G).

i.e. $Y = C + I + G$ equation (i)

Now $Yd = (1 - t) Y$

Since the tax rate (t) is 25%, disposable income (Yd) is three-quarters of total income

$$\therefore \quad Yd \ = \ \frac{3}{4}Y$$

Substituting into the consumption function :

$$C \quad = \ 3 + \frac{4}{5} \cdot \frac{3}{4}Y$$

$$\therefore \quad C = \ = \ 3 + \frac{3}{5}Y$$

Substituting in equation (i) :

$$Y = \ 3 + \frac{3}{5}Y + 5 + 8$$

$$\therefore \ (1 - \frac{3}{5})Y \ = \ 16$$

$$\therefore \ Y \ = \ \frac{5}{2} \times 16 = \ \underline{£40 \ m} \ \text{the equilibrium level of income.}$$

b)   The full employment level of income is £50 m. Thus an increase of £10 m is required to achieve full employment equilibrium.

(i)   Let the level of government expenditure required to achieve full employment be G_1

Then from equation (i)

$$50 = 3 + \frac{3}{5} \times 50 + 5 + G_1$$

$$\therefore \underline{G_1 = £12 \text{ m}}$$

(ii)   Let the tax rate required to achieve full employment equilibrium be t_1, then :

$$50 = 3 + \frac{4}{5}(1 - t_1) 50 + 5 + 8$$

$$\therefore 34 = 40 - 40t_1$$

$$\therefore \underline{t_1 = \frac{3}{20}}$$

Thus if either government expenditure is raised to £12 m, or the tax rate lowered to $\frac{3}{20}$, full employment equilibrium will be achieved.

Answer 14

a)   The total demand for money (Md) is composed of two elements : the demand for active balances (Ma) and the demand for idle balances (Mi). In equilibrium demand equals supply

i.e.   Md = Ms

$\therefore$ Ma + Mi = Ms

Now $Ma = \frac{1}{3}Y$

when   Y = £2400 m

$$Ma = \frac{1}{3} \times 2400 = £800$$

$\therefore$ in equilibrium   Mi = Ms - Ma

$$= 1600 - 800$$

$$= £800 \text{ m}$$

From the given schedule the demand for idle balances is £800 m when the interest rate is 14%.

b)   In equilibrium

$$Ms = Ma + Mi$$

when $Y = 3000$

$$Ma = \frac{1}{3} \times 3000 = £1000 \text{ m}$$

If $r = 10\%$

then $Mi = £1000 \text{ m}$

∴ required value of the money supply is Ma + Mi

∴ $Ms = 1000 + 1000 = \underline{£2,000 \text{ m}}$

Answer 15

a) The gains from trade are based on differences in opportunity costs. These costs of producing one unit of each commodity in terms of the other may be summarized in the following table

Country	Opportunity cost of X in terms of Y	Opportunity cost of Y in terms of X
A	10Y	$\frac{1}{10}X$
B	3Y	$\frac{1}{3}X$

Thus A has a comparative advantage in the production of Y and a comparative disadvantage in producing X.

Suppose prior to trade both countries produce both commodities. Now if A increases its production of Y by one unit (by reducing output of X by $\frac{1}{10}$ unit and B decreases its production of Y by one unit (and uses the freed resources to produce an extra $\frac{1}{3}$ unit of X), then overall output of Y remains constamt, while output of X is raised by $(\frac{1}{3} - \frac{1}{10})$ unit, i.e. $\frac{7}{30}$ unit. This additional output may then be distributed between the two countries enabling them both to gain from trade. Greater specialisation would reap even greater gains.

b)   In country A the opportunity cost of producing one unit of X is 10Y. If it can obtain one unit of X from trade at a lower cost it will prefer to trade for X, rather than produce it directly.

In country B the opportunity cost of producing X is 3Y. Thus if it can obtain more than 3Y by trading one unit of X it will prefer to trade for Y, rather than produce it directly.

Therefore trade will take place provided the rate of exchange for one unit of X lies between 10 and 3 units of Y.

Appendix 2

Preparation for Economics Examinations

Contents. (1) Study efficiently
(2) Plans and timetables
(3) A suggested method of study
(4) Examinations.

(1) Study efficiently

You have embarked on an examinable course in Economics. Success in this venture will depend not only on ability and hard work but also on how efficiently you can study. It is much easier to understand economics if you work in a sustained and systematic manner. Such concentration of effort requires a high degree of motivation - due perhaps to a definite vocational goal or a strong interest in the subject matter. One hour's concentrated study on a particularly interesting topic may accomplish more than an evening's disinterested browsing through a text-book. The following list are suggestions for raising your level of motivation and hence ability to work effectively:

a)   Develop an interest in the subject by reading the economic commentaries in the quality papers and commercial bank reviews, to see how economic forces affect our daily lives.

b)   Do not allow your attention to wander during periods of study by eliminating (as far as possible) all sources of distraction.

c)   Set yourself a reasonable task to complete by a certain time. This may involve reading and taking notes on a particular chapter in your text-book, or writing an essay.

d)   Try to obtain as much information as you can about your progress in the subject by discussing essays and questions (including your errors and omissions) with your tutor.

e)   If you have time, read around your subject. Economics is a relatively young social science and there are many instances of 'great debates' among different schools of thought where the prevailing wisdom was challenged by alternative views. The methods outlined in your text-book may not be the 'only' way of analysing a problem.

(2) Plans and timetables

A common obstacle to success is the lack of a plan of study. Such a plan is essential if you are to cover the syllabus properly. A rigid timetable is not usually a good idea but you must set yourself a certain feasible number of hours study-time per week. Get a copy of the syllabus for your course, and with the aid of a good text book break down the contents into manageable proportions which you think you will be able to cope with in a certain period, say one week. This will provide you with an overall view of your work load. Then at the beginning of each week you can construct a time-table for the work for that particular week. Allow yourself plenty of time to finish your plan of studies before the examination date - you will need to devote between six and eight weeks to revision prior to sitting the examination.

During each weekly section of your work plan set yourself time constraints for completing certain pieces of work and try your best to keep to them. Practice working under time pressure now and it will pay off later during the examination. Keeping to a plan or time-table is largely a matter of habit, so set aside certain times for study in a reasonably quiet environment away from outside distraction. Start work immediately you sit down and do not wait for inspiration - it rarely comes. The length of an individual study session varies considerably among students, with the average between two and three hours.

(3) A suggested method of study

If you have difficulty in organising your own methods of study, or have no particular way of learning new material, you may like to try a study system used in the U.S.A., called SQ3R. The SQ3R stands for: Survey, Questions, Read, Recite, Revise.

a) Survey: all too often a student attempts to learn particular techniques without understanding why or how they are relevant to his course of study. It is very important when beginning a topic to obtain an overall perspective. For example, most students can manage to grasp fairly quickly the technique of finding the equilibrium level of national income via the Keynesian cross diagram, but few understand the actual importance of the existence of such an equilibrium level to government policy or its limitations. Therefore before you begin a new topic make a point of surveying the whole area to see how each item relates to the whole.

b)   Question: adopt an inquisitive attitude during your initial survey. Make a point of writing down questions that occur to you. How does the new material impinge on your existing body of knowledge? For example how does international trade affect the pre-trade equilibrium level of national income?

c)   Reading: read thoroughly over the material to be covered, making particular notes concerning diagrams and other illustrations of the verbal argument. Keep your initial survey in mind as you read so you are able to place each argument in its proper context - this is very important. If necessary re-read a previous section to remind yourself of an important point which you need for the current analysis.

d)   Recitation: after reading each new topic or major section from your text-book or lecture notes, lay the book down and try to recall the key ideas. You may find it useful to jot down in note form what you remember. Now go over the material again and check whether your notes (and memory) are accurate. You may need to read a section four or five times before you can recall all the material properly.

e)   Revision: the first revision of new material should take place fairly soon after the initial learning. This helps to strengthen your memory of the topic considerably. A good way to revise is to consult an alternative text-book to reinforce your knowledge. This may also help to provide additional points or new insights which were not fully discussed previously. Some subsequent revision is necessary before completing a piece of work such as an essay. A final revision period of between six and eight weeks before the examination is necessary to enable you to go over all the material again, paying particular attention to earlier topics which may have been forgotten.

During each stage of the study method it is vitally important that you make notes to which you can refer later. When you have completed the first revision of the material you should be able to organise your notes into a logical framework, making any additions or corrections as necessary. This will save you considerable time during the final revision, and provide you with an excellent subject reference base.

(4) Examinations

Initial preparation for an examination begins at the start of your course. You should determine the extent of the material to be covered, preferably by obtaining a copy of the syllabus. Choose a good text-book. If there are several possible choices, have a glance through them all to decide which style of writing and presentation suits you best. Find out all you can about the conditions of the examination; how many papers you must take, how long each paper is, how many questions you must answer, what choice of questions is offered, how many marks may be obtained for each question or section.

If you have organised your studies efficiently you should begin your final revision period for the examination with a concise set of notes covering the syllabus. Your next task is to identify key areas of the course which will form the basis for examination questions. These key areas do vary among examining bodies but most inter-mediate papers in Economics include questions on the following topics:

a) Demand and Supply, including elasticity, effects of taxes and price controls.

b) Theory of the firm, organisation, finance and objectives.

c) Cost curves.

d) Optimal factor mix, returns to scale, returns to a factor.

e) Market structures, perfect competition, monopoly, imperfect competition.

f) National Income Accounting.

g) Equilibrium level of National Income.

h) Multipliers and fiscal policy.

i) Demand for and supply of money, rate of interest, monetary policy.

j) International trade, comparative advantage, exchange rates, Balance of Payments.

k) Inflation and unemployment.

Try to obtain past examination papers and use these in conjunction with those in this book to give a rough indication of what to expect in an examination. Practice answering questions under time con-straints continually during the course, and compare your answer with the model answer, if necessary rewriting incorrect passages. Make a point of learning from previous errors or omissions and strive not to make the same mistake twice.

In the days before the examination do not resort to cramming which is usually a last despairing effort to learn material which should have been covered months ago. Burning the midnight oil only leaves you mentally and physically fatigued. Aim to arrange your revision and non-academic affairs so that you are mentally alert and physically fit as you enter the exam room - <u>not</u> tired and haggered. Give yourself plenty of time to reach the room where the examination is to be held and make sure you have all the necessary equipment to hand: ruler, pen, pencil, rubber, etc.

Once in the examination room read through the paper thoroughly and construct a rough timetable, e.g. if you are asked to answer five questions in three hours you should spend 30-35 minutes per question, allowing approximately 10 minutes initial reading of the paper and 10 minutes final reading through your answers.

If you have a choice of questions then during your preliminary reading of the paper you should indicate which questions you feel competent to answer. Make a final choice of questions to be answered, picking those questions from your list of 'possibles' that you feel most confident about. Your best questions should be attempted first. Make sure you understand every part of the question and what is required from you before attempting an answer. In essay-type questions construct a plan: first note down points you intend to use and then structure them into a logical framework, possibly adding an introductory paragraph and a conclusion. Remember that diagrams can convey much information quickly and efficiently - but they must be drawn accurately - so use a ruler for all straight lines. Try to keep to your timetable and do not spend too long on one question - diminishing returns quickly set in. Write legibly, in some examinations bad handwriting is penalised. If you succeed in meeting your time constraints you should have time at the end to reread your answers and add final touches to your diagrams and other illustrations.